FERRY & CRUISE

annual
2012

Published by:

Ferry Publications, PO Box 33, Ramsey, Isle of Man IM99 4LP

Tel: +44 (0) 1624 898445   Fax: +44 (0) 1624 898449

E-mail: ferrypubs@manx.net   Website: www.ferrypubs.co.uk

Ferry
Publications

CONTENTS

Introduction

Edition 4 of our increasingly popular 'Ferry & Cruise Annual' brings more specially commissioned articles and high-quality photographs to our growing readership.

Our lead article concerns the final Sealink 'Saint' which, after having long outlived her half sisters, was finally withdrawn from service on the Stranraer-Belfast service in 2011. As the *St David*, and latterly the *Stena Caledonia*, the thirty-year old vessel was the last major build for the nationalised railway fleet and the last to remain in UK service. She was also a link with the famous Harland & Wolff yard at Belfast which this year also marks the centenary of perhaps its most famous ship.

Other contributions involve the growth of the sea routes to the Scottish island of Islay as the introduction of the new *Finlaggan* is duly marked. Elsewhere we look at the efforts to save the former Isle of Man Steam Packet Company's passenger steamer *Manxman* as seen through the eyes of one of the directors of the company formed to try and keep her from the breakers' torch. Small ferries are not forgotten and a record of the diminutive Gosport fleets is provided. These fascinating workhorses

mostly enjoyed long lives and frequently served as excursion vessels following their withdrawal. A further ferry-based article concerns the myriad of ro-ro services in the Baltic which frequently fail to be given the coverage which they deserve.

The cruise aspect of the annual looks at the popular P&O twins *Oriana* and *Aurora* 'truly British superliners' while another piece looks at the life and career of a Purser at Sea. We go to sea on board the *Ocean Pearl* and *Le Boreal* and also sail around the British Isles in Fred. Olsen's *Black Watch*.

Finally there are photographic interludes which involve the ships of Norway's legendary inside passage, the growing cruise fleet operated by Saga Cruises and a wonderful wallow in nostalgia as we look at some iconic liners of the past from the FotoFlite collection.

As usual, we hope that there will be something for everyone within these covers. Edition 5 is already under way!

John Hendy & Miles Cowsill
November 2011

Seen in the Baltic during June 2010, DSB's Urd was built in Italy in 1981 as the Easy Rider. Arrested and laid up in Greece two years later, in 1985 she was purchased by Sealink British Ferries (along with her sister Lucky Rider/Seafreight Freeway) and in 1987 was renamed Seafreight Highway for service from Dover to Zeebrugge. Once again she failed to establish herself and was subsequently sold to Bulgarian owners in 1988 before a further sale to Denmark in 1990. Since then she has seen a variety of routes and during 2010 was in operation between Travemunde and Ventspils (Latvia). (John Hendy)

1 Stena Caledonia – Sealink's Last Saint

by Scott Mackey

SAINT CLASS – THE BELFAST SISTERS

Part of the UK ferry scene for three decades and mainstay of Stranraer's ferry link with Northern Ireland for 25 years, the *Stena Caledonia* was built as the *St David*, the final vessel in a series of four car ferries ordered by the British Railways Board for Sealink from the Belfast yard of Harland and Wolff in the late 1970s. The first ship, *Galloway Princess* (yard number 1713) was destined for service on the Larne to Stranraer route and, despite a delay of some ten months, revolutionised the service when she entered service in May 1980. With her twin-level bow and stern loading, capacity for 62 trailers or 280 cars and up to 1,000 passengers, the 'Galloway' was like nothing ever seen before on the North Channel. She faithfully served the Scottish port of Stranraer's links with Northern Ireland for 22 years before being sold for further service in the Straits of Gibraltar as IMTC's *Le Rif* in 2002.

The second and third vessels in the series that was later to become known as the 'Saint' Class were destined for the Flagship route between Dover and Calais. The *St Anselm* (yard number 1715) and *St Christopher*

(yard number 1716) were to be part of a three-ship line up which was completed by SNCF's *Cote d'Azur*, a vessel of similar size constructed in France and which made up the French partnership's contingent on the route. Again, these vessels were delayed by some ten months, with the *St Christopher* even being redirected to complete her maiden voyage between Holyhead and Dun Laoghaire in March 1981, before debuting at Dover in mid-April.

The sisters returned to Belfast for modifications which involved the enlarging of their passenger accommodation in 1983 and served the Dover to Calais route together until 1990 when the *St Anselm* was moved to Folkestone and, thus to Holyhead as the *Stena Cambria* in 1991. The *St Christopher* was renamed *Stena Antrim* and took up service on the Larne to Stranraer route in time for the summer season of 1991, where she joined erstwhile sister vessels, *Galloway Princess*, by then renamed *Stena Galloway* and *St David*, renamed *Stena Caledonia*.

The *Stena Cambria* and the *Stena Antrim* both saw a return to service on the English Channel in the mid-1990s, operating from Dover and

*A fine view of the **St David** captured early in her career, in her original Sealink livery at speed. Her somewhat austere but very functional design is very apparent in this image. (FotoFlite)*

*Large crowds gather to see the fourth vessel in the 'Saint' Class series, **St David**, enter the water for the first time at the Harland and Wolff Shipyard, Belfast on 25th September 1980. She was the final ship to be built at H&W's Musgrave yard and, indeed, the last passenger vessel built in Belfast. (Ferry Publications Library)*

Newhaven before being sold off for further service in the Mediterranean, as *Isla de Botafoc* for Umafisa (later Balearia) and *Ibn Batouta* for Limadet (later Comanav) respectively. The 'Cambria' was sold again in early 2010, initially destined for the scrap man's torch, but she was afforded a reprieve and now operates for Ventouris Ferries of Greece as the *Bari*.

DESIGN

The somewhat functional appearance of the sisters was, to many, in stark contrast to the unusual yet modern appearance of Townsend Thoresen's 'Spirit' Class, built in Germany around the same time. They were, however, somewhat different to anything ever built before for Sealink – featuring twin funnels on either side of the hull, allowing two unobstructed vehicle decks through which traffic could drive on and off through bow and stern doors without the need for manoeuvring. Moreover, the majority of accommodation on all four ships was concentrated on one deck (Deck 7), with additional spaces afforded towards the aft end of Deck 8.

Sealink's Naval Architects at the time, Don Ripley and Tony Rogan were given a brief to provide ships which would be suitable for use at the majority of the company's ports, both provided with double deck or single deck linkspans. Despite the somewhat austere profile of the Saints, their design was indeed, in many ways, ahead of their time and the requirements of the operator were met with an innovative solution which allowed for double or single deck loading and discharging where vehicles could be driven directly into position on both cargo decks. The ships were also the first vessels in the Sealink fleet to feature hydraulic deck equipment.

The layout of the *St David*'s passenger accommodation areas was somewhat different to her three sisters. She was designed for longer Irish Sea crossings and, thus, featured a smaller restaurant located forward, a cinema, a supermarket and the lounge bar located on the upper deck.

The *St David* was also built with a stern bridge for astern manoeuvring at Holyhead's inner harbour. This feature always made sure she was instantly recognisable and stood out from her near sisters. Following the move from Larne to Belfast in 1995 which involved much astern navigation up the River Lagan towards her berth, this was never used and has since been completely stripped out with many of the parts being used for spares as these became more difficult to source in more recent years.

ON BOARD

The majority of the 'Caledonia's' passenger accommodation is situated on Deck 7. The ship's superstructure extends to the edge of the hull just forward and aft of the two centrally located twin funnels. Forward to starboard is the galley, with the Trucker's Lounge to port. The Food City buffet restaurant is situated just aft of these, from where we continue aft into the main body of the ship's accommodation.

Captured early in her now lengthy UK career, the **St David,** *makes a fine sight at sea with her promenade decks lined with passengers. (FotoFlite)*

The St David is dressed overall on the occasion of her first arrival at Holyhead, direct from her Belfast builders, on 5th August 1981. (John Marsh, courtesy Capt Ray Veno. Justin Merrigan Collection)

Moving astern off the berth at Fishguard, St David's bow visor is lowered during one of her spells of service on the St George's Channel service to Rosslare in the early 1980s. (Miles Cowsill)

Following privatisation in 1984, the St David shows off the recently adopted livery of Sealink British Ferries on arrival at Fishguard in the mid-1980s. (Miles Cowsill)

This features a large open plan lounge which was created by the removal of dividing bulwarks in 2009. In the centre of this lounge is the Barista Coffee House and Bar surrounded by a selection of seating types, from fixed sofas to armchairs and tables. Guest Services is located centrally towards the centre of the ship, adjacent to the main lounge and the exclusive premium Stena Plus lounge which seats around 40, located enclosed to starboard.

Continuing aft, a Curious George Children's play area, video warp gaming area and enclosed slot machine zone lead to Stena Shopping right aft to port and the Cinema starboard. On Deck 8, the Sports Bar aft is available for seating on all sailings, although the bar itself is only open on selected sailings. Just forward of the sports bar was formerly a quiet lounge area, including a cafe servery which very seldom if ever saw the light of day at Stranraer.

This area was re-carpeted and re-upholstered along with the rest of the ship in 2009, but in early 2010, the decision was taken to create an additional Stena Plus facility for families in this area. This is a very pleasant area with a cordoned off outside deck area adjacent on both the starboard and port sides.

The 'Caledonia's' facilities are broadly in line with other Stena Line ships, albeit now on a smaller scale than most. She normally operates with a passenger certificate level of 664 which can be increased accordingly to a maximum of 1,000.

THREE DECADES OF SERVICE

While her three sisters have since left UK waters for warmer climes, the fourth ship in the series finally completed service in October 2011 on the key Northern Ireland to Scotland link between Belfast, the place of her birth, and Stranraer as the *Stena Caledonia*.

The keel of yard number 1717 was laid at Harland and Wolff on 14th December 1979, with her launch taking place from Musgrave Yard Slipway number 8 on 25th September 1980. Christened by Mrs Derrick Fowler, she was the last ship to be launched from Harland and Wolff's Musgrave Yard and entered service on 10th August 1981 between Holyhead and Dun Laoghaire. During her first winter in service, it was decided by local management at Holyhead that the *St David* would operate the route instead of the *St Columba*. The latter ship had a much more significant capacity for passengers but did not have the space for as much freight. It was, therefore, felt that the *St David* provided the route with a much more viable and economic option to work the service during the off-peak winter months.

During March 1982, the *St David* was prevented from entering Dun Laoghaire harbour by protesting B&I Line crews who used their vessel, *Munster*, to block the port entrance. The blockade was in response to a similar reception encountered by the Irish at Holyhead when they attempted to inaugurate a service between Anglesey and Dublin. In 1983, the *St David* covered overhauls at Stranraer for the first time and then sailed south to cover on the Fishguard service, before filling in for sisters, *St Anselm* and *St Christopher* at Dover while they returned to Belfast for modifications to their accommodation, mainly involving extensions to their main passenger deck aft over the poop deck.

Following some three months at the Kent port, working alongside SNCF's *Champs Elysees* (later to become *Stena Navigator* and partner the 'Caledonia' on the North Channel), the *St David* returned to Holyhead to resume service for the remainder of the year, in tandem with the *St Columba*. In 1984 she was again used to cover refits at Stranraer, but also saw surprise service at Harwich in lieu of the *St Nicholas* for three weeks. The *St*

*The **St David** is pictured in dry dock at Swansea Shipyard for her annual overhaul in 1986. (Miles Cowsill)*

*Lying over in Dover's Western Docks during 1985, the **St David** undergoes preparation for her short-lived stint on the Ostend service which was brought to a rather abrupt end after a disagreement between Sealink British Ferries and their Belgian Partners, RTM. (Miles Cowsill)*

*Above & Below: Two fine views of the **Stena Caledonia** leaving the County Antrim port of Larne on a beautiful sunny day. A few short years later, the Northern Irish port was moved to a purpose-built facility on the River Lagan in Belfast Harbour, bringing an end to the historic link between Larne and Stranraer. (Miles Cowsill)*

Wearing Stena Line colours, the **Stena Caledonia** *speeds past Cairnryan outward bound in Loch Ryan on a sailing from Stranraer to Belfast in 1996. (Miles Cowsill)*

Wednesday 10th August 2011 and the **Stena Caledonia** *is photographed in the scenic beauty of Loch Ryan on a well-loaded sailing to Belfast. This was the occasion of the 30th anniversary of her entry into service at Holyhead in 1981. (Gordon Hislip)*

A beautiful summer's day in Loch Ryan and the **Stena Navigator** (ex **Champs Elysees**, **Stena Parisien**, **SeaFrance Manet**) is inward bound to Stranraer, passing the **Stena Caledonia** on her morning sailing to Belfast. (Miles Cowsill)

Viewed from the bridge, the **Stena Caledonia** is assisted out of dry dock by tugboat, **Smit Waterloo** at the yard of Cammell Laird, Birkenhead following her 2009 refit and major accommodation refurbishment. (Captain Murray Paterson)

David operated the Dutch service mainly as a freight vessel, operating alongside *Koningin Juliana*.

The following year, along with all other ships in the Sealink fleet, the *St David* lost her blue hull in favour of the new colours to be adopted by Sealink British Ferries following privatisation and take over by Sea Containers. The year 1985 was, perhaps, also the most eventful year of the ship's career. She was due to be transferred to Dover in March to operate to Ostend, a joint partnership service with RTM, alongside their *Stena Nautica* and *Reine Astrid*. During this time she also operated to Boulogne during the summer months on Saturdays. A disagreement with the Belgians when Sea Containers wanted greater involvement in the Ostend route saw the *St David* and Sealink banned from operating to Belgium. The *St David* then returned to the Irish Sea and covered at Holyhead before she finally found a permanent home at the Scottish port of Stranraer in 1986.

Despite now being settled in her new home, the ship still proved her reputation for flexibility and reliability by continuing to provide annual cover for fleet overhauls at Holyhead and Fishguard. The next few settled years saw the *St David* and *Galloway Princess* maintain the key rosters on the Larne to Stranraer service with the *Darnia* as third ship. During this time, the two sister vessels were instrumental in building passenger and freight traffic numbers on the North Channel service.

When Stena Line purchased Sealink British Ferries in 1990, the *St David* was given a truly local name, with reminders of the days of the *Caledonian Princess* when she became the *Stena Caledonia* and her port of registry was changed to Stranraer. Her suitability for the route and that of her partner and older sister, the *Galloway Princess* was underlined when she was herself replaced by a series of unsuitable vessels during annual refit periods. In 1991, the *Darnia* was replaced by *St Christopher*, by now renamed *Stena Antrim*, and the route was in the hands of three of the four sisters, providing an unrivalled service operated by three broadly similar vessels allowing great levels of flexibility and standards of service unequalled on the Northern Ireland-Scotland link.

In the intervening years, the Larne service was moved to Belfast in 1995 and all four of the Harland and Wolff sisters saw periods of service from the city in which they were built at one stage or another. The remaining sister, *St Anselm*, was by now the *Stena Cambria* and was a regular vessel on the Holyhead route as well as seeing stints on the Stranraer link covering for one or other of her sisters on various occasions. She was the only sister to see service from Larne in full Stena Line colours, prior to the transfer to new facilities just opposite the shipyard on the River Lagan in Belfast.

Following the introduction of the second HSS, the *Stena Voyager*, the *Stena Antrim* was maintained for a short time as back-up ship, before moving to join the *Stena Cambria* at Newhaven. The *Galloway Princess* was, by now, the *Stena Galloway* and operated the Belfast to Stranraer service faithfully alongside her younger sister, *Stena Caledonia* in back-up to the *Stena Voyager* HSS from 1996 until her sale to Morocco in 2002. The two sisters provided a back-up service carrying mainly freight while the HSS absorbed virtually all the tourist traffic on the route.

In July 1999, the 'Caledonia' joined fleet mates, *Stena Challenger* and *Koningin Beatrix* to convey support teams and crews from Rosslare to Roscoff for the Tour de France cycle race. Between them, the three ships carried over 2,000 personnel, television and media crews, cars, vans, lorries and a hospitality unit. Tentative plans to return to Larne with the conventional vessels, *Stena Caledonia* and *Stena Galloway* in 2000 saw Captain Murray Paterson take the ship into what was once familiar territory for berthing trials in October 1999. The ships were, however, never to return

The **Stena Caledonia**'s *unique and very flexible vehicle deck ramp arrangement is illustrated by this view during her annual refit at Harland and Wolff in March 2011. The entire upper level is suspended and hinged, allowing vehicles to use both decks at either a single or double-deck shore linkspan. (Scott Mackey)*

A stormy Belfast Lough in November 2010 and the **Stena Caledonia** *approaches her berth at Victoria Terminal 4 on another crossing from Stranraer. (Scott Mackey)*

Underneath the **Stena Caledonia** *in dry dock at Harland and Wolff during her final Stena Line refit in March 2011 with the ship's twin semi-spade rudders and twin 4-blade variable pitch propellers receiving attention. (Scott Mackey)*

A view of the **Stena Caledonia**'*s Bridge while alongside at her Victoria Terminal 4 berth in Belfast, looking across to starboard in May 2011. (Scott Mackey).*

The **Stena Caledonia**'*s main engine room in July 2010 and one of the ship's 2 x 7675 kW Pielstick engines is seen to good advantage. (Scott Mackey)*

to the County Antrim port and continued operating to and from Belfast.

The 'Caledonia' spent six weeks at refit on the Mersey in 2000 when she emerged with an altered and slightly elongated profile, consisting of so-called 'duck tail' type sponsons at her stern and a new bulbous bow in place of her original bow rudder. While these modifications did little for her aesthetically, they have definitely given the ship an increased lifespan while also conforming to enhanced SOLAS regulations and the Stockholm Agreement. During this time, the vessel was also fitted with dividing doors on her main vehicle deck.

An almost unbroken seven years of service at Stranraer ended in 2005 when the 'Caledonia' was, once again, covering at Rosslare while the *Stena Europe* went for overhaul. The 'Caledonia' was, in turn, replaced by Fleetwood's third ship, the *Stena Seafarer* – the first time this vessel had operated the Scottish service. The 'Seafarer' has continued to provide refit cover for the 'Caledonia' every year since and has also been used to cover the *Stena Navigator*'s overhauls. In more recent years, the 'Caledonia' has not been used to cover other fleet refits, further emphasising her re-emerging importance as a key vessel on the Belfast to Stranraer service. Instead, the *Stena Seafarer* has made a few trips south to Rosslare to cover for the *Stena Europe*.

The introduction of the Finnish-built HSS *Stena Voyager* at Stranraer in 1996 was set to revolutionise the ferry industry. Many believed that such vessels would, ultimately lead to the demise of the *Stena Caledonia* and similar vessels. For years, passengers were actively persuaded to use the HSS, with the *Stena Caledonia* retained for mainly a freight and back-up role. While her sister, the *Stena Galloway*, was sacrificed to the Moroccans in support of efforts to make the HSS work in 2002, the high operating costs of the *Stena Voyager* were always to be her downfall. A move downstream to a brand new purpose-built facility at Victoria Terminal 4 at the edge of the port of Belfast, reduced journey distances for both the HSS and conventional operation, while the opportunity was taken to slow the HSS down while still maintaining the same crossing duration. The 'Caledonia's' sailings, however, were reduced by some 15 minutes in duration as a result of this move in 2008 and this coincided with a reduction in the *Stena Voyager*'s schedule from five to four daily round trips. This reduction saw the 'Caledonia' used more intensively, especially on night time sailings where she was required to operate with turn-around times of as little as 45-60 minutes. She also saw increased summer and weekend daytime service, providing extra capacity in light of fewer fast sailings.

Global financial circumstances and rising fuel costs mean that Stena's HSS concept will be outlived by the likes of the 'Caledonia', albeit only for a short while, and this was emphasised as the 'Voyager' will not feature in the company's plans following their move out of Stranraer to the new Loch Ryan Port, north of Cairnryan in Autumn 2011. Indeed, it was announced in March 2011 that the 'Caledonia' and 'Navigator' will be replaced on the route by chartered sisters *Superfast VII* and *Superfast VIII* from November.

Reinforcing the 'Caledonia's' position at the forefront of operations on the North Channel, the ship benefitted from a major overhaul and refurbishment in her 28th year, 2009. The accommodation areas had not been changed since the early 1990s and, despite being in spotless condition (mainly due to the fact that they were hugely underused, but also due to the high standards of maintenance applied by her dedicated crew) the redesign of the main passenger areas on Deck 7 by Figura Arkitekter and refurbishment work carried out by County Down based MJM Marine transformed the ship and brought her into line with facilities on a par with many of her larger and much more modern fleet mates. The company's

A view across to starboard in the **Stena Caledonia**'s Food City Restaurant, located forward on Deck 7. (Miles Cowsill)

One of the **Stena Caledonia**'s two premium Stena Plus lounges in 2011. This is the lounge on Deck 7, complete with borrowed seats from the by-now-redundant **Stena Seafarer** while the 'Caledonia's' own seats underwent repairs. (Miles Cowsill)

Looking aft towards towards the retail complex from the after end of the **Stena Caledonia**'s main lounge and Barista Coffee House on Deck 7. (Miles Cowsill)

With the Barista Coffee House on the left, this view is starboard looking forward in the **Stena Caledonia**'s main lounge area on Deck 7. (Miles Cowsill)

An overall view looking forward in the **Stena Caledonia**'s Food City Restaurant located forward on Deck 7. (Miles Cowsill)

Although refurbished in 2009, the servery area of Food City on the **Stena Caledonia** retains the same layout introduced with the Pantry Restaurant by Sealink British Ferries in 1986. (Miles Cowsill)

'Making Good Time' for Stranraer as the **Stena Caledonia** *departs Belfast on a routine crossing in the summer of 2011. (Miles Cowsill)*

The **Stena Caledonia** *arrives in Loch Ryan en route to Stranraer and displays the latest version of the Stena Line livery to good advantage in the summer sunshine. (Miles Cowsill)*

Loading vehicles onto the upper deck of the **Stena Caledonia** at Victoria Terminal 4 in Belfast. (Stena Line)

concentration on conventional ferries and shift away from the HSS was further underpinned by the purchase of the *SeaFrance Manet* (*ex Champs Elysees*), a ship of similar size and vintage (built 1984) for the route and her entry into service as the *Stena Navigator* following a major internal overhaul in November 2009. The *Stena Caledonia* has continued to benefit from accommodation enhancements in 2010 with the refurbishment of an area on Deck 8 to comprise an additional premium Stena Plus lounge.

SERVICE IN THE 21ST CENTURY

Under the dedicated and faithful leadership of Senior Master, Captain Murray Paterson since 2001, the *Stena Caledonia* has faithfully served Stranraer now for some 25 years and operated in and out of Belfast since late 1995. The flexible design and ease of operation of the ship saw her continue to visit Rosslare and Fishguard in recent years as well as two successful charters to the Isle of Man Steam Packet Company during the TT period in 2007 and 2008, operating into Douglas and Heysham. Captain Paul Williams joined the ship in 1986 and spoke highly of his charge and her ease of operation, flexibility and high levels of manoeuvrability. That she remained highly suitable for the purpose for which she was built, he claimed, is testament to her design, construction and the standard of maintenance afforded by her team of dedicated engineers under the guidance of Senior Chief Engineer Gary Muncaster, deck crew, on-board services crew and officers.

Senior Master Paterson is particularly proud of the fact that the 'Caledonia' had faithfully maintained the link between Northern Ireland and Scotland in all but the very worst weather conditions and was frequently called upon to help out when the HSS was unable to sail. She was, in fact, often referred to as "old reliable" and, he claims, could take pretty much everything the North Channel could throw at her. "Both men agree that they don't build them like this anymore and that the standard of construction is second-to-none. Much credit must go to Gary Muncaster and several of his engineering team without whom, this elderly lady wouldn't have been reliably plying the North Channel after three decades.

To say the 'Caledonia' was innovative or perhaps even a ro-pax before her time is something Senior Master Paterson and Captain Williams would agree with. Her ability to swallow two full vehicle deck loads over a two-tier shore ramp or even with the use of her revolutionary internal ramps in ports where only a single-level linkspan was available, have proved their worth throughout the ships life from the early days at Holyhead to her

recent visits to Heysham and Douglas. Many onboard expressed their delight the ship had been returned to full passenger service in late 2009. For a number of years most daylight hours were spent alongside in Belfast while the HSS swallowed virtually all tourist traffic. The 'Caledonia' was mainly reserved for night time sailings which mostly carried freight. Many of the crew claimed that being tied up in Belfast most days was a "bit boring" and while it was good for maintenance purposes "there's only so many times you can paint something!" Undoubtedly those years spent on the sidelines are the reason the 'Caledonia' has remained so well maintained.

On-board Services Co-ordinator, Martin Kearney is certainly very particular about the standard of maintenance and cleanliness of the accommodation areas – so much so that he proudly pointed out that he believes their ship was probably the cleanest in the fleet. Clearly, a return to full passenger service on the lead rota in November 2009 placed new demands on the ageing ship and her crew, but they rose to the challenge admirably. The 'Caledonia' latterly operated with a crew of 50, 25 day and 25 night, working 12-hour shifts and living on board for one week from Wednesday to Wednesday, with one week off in between.

Senior Master, Captain Murray Paterson served on all four of the Belfast sisters and joined the 'Caledonia' in 1995, becoming Senior Master in 2001. He spoke enthusiastically about his charge and the team of dedicated crew members charged with keeping the ship in tip-top condition and of how she will be missed. The ship's team was one for which he had the highest praise and he believed that the level of dedication and professionalism displayed by all on board the 'Caledonia' meant that they were well placed to meet the challenges posed by the introduction of new tonnage on the route, later in 2011.

ANNIVERSARY

Remarkable because three decades later the vessel had continued to reliably traffic the Irish Sea for which she was built. Remarkable because the ship quietly slipped in and out of Belfast day-in and day-out, in the shadow of the great shipyard where she was built. Remarkable because the ship has been kept in pristine condition by her proud and dedicated crew and offered passengers service that is truly second-to-none. Remarkable because the flexible and highly innovative design of her and her near sisters meant that she was still highly suitable for the route she trafficed so reliably since becoming a regular Stranraer ship 25 years ago. Remarkable because the *Stena Caledonia* was the last Sealink ship still in operation in the UK, the last of the four so-called 'Saint' class vessels still serving routes she was originally designed and built for, the last passenger ship built by Harland and Wolff and the last and only remaining truly local ferry.

After an extremely noteworthy three decades of service for what is basically the same operator, the *Stena Caledonia* was retired from Stena Line service in mid-November 2011. Her final few weeks in service were not without their problems. Technical issues with the *Stena Navigator* and weather related problems meant that 'old reliable' was called upon on a number of occasions to prove her worth.

This grand old lady will be missed by many people, but more keenly by those who have been directly involved with the *St David / Stena Caledonia* over the years, but it surely can be said that this rather ordinary but extremely remarkable little (by today's standards) ferry has served her purpose well.

A final word from Senior Master, Captain Murray Paterson - "Hail Caledonia, a fine British ship!"

2

Oriana & Aurora – Truly British Cruise Ships

by Brian David Smith

The *Oriana* and *Aurora* are truly British Superliners. Built for P&O Cruises by the German Shipyard of Meyer Werft in 1995 and 2000 respectively, they are the only large passenger ships designed and built exclusively for the British market. With their beautifully looking raked sterns, expansive outside deck space and gleaming white hulls they are instantly recognisable anywhere in the world. However, in the five years between the two ships entering service, the lessons learned from the *Oriana*'s design combined with a complete revamp of the company's technical department, meant that the two ships are actually incredibly different.

ORIANA

When the *Oriana* entered service in April 2005, she was the first new build for P&O since the popular *Canberra* had entered service in 1961. An innovative design with her funnel and machinery placed aft to create more passenger space and open interior spaces, her flowing superstructure allowed for a large amount of open deck space which is a feature of any successful British cruise ship. Originally designed for the Australian run, she entered service as a two-class ship but in 1974 was converted to a one-class cruise ship for just over 1,700 passengers. At one point she was P&O's only vessel in service but had built up a very loyal following of passengers. Despite this, it was clear towards the end of the 1980s that the *Canberra* was going to need replacing before the end of the century and a team was put together to build Britain's first new large passenger ship since the 'QE2'.

Under the project name of Gemini, a team was assembled to put to work designing the general arrangement which shipyards would be invited to tender. The project manager was James Hunter. His naval architects for the project were led by Richard Vie with the interior design by the Swedish architect Robert Tillberg. Their brief was to design a ship with a capacity of around 2,000 passengers, to look at the *Canberra* and use what worked well and improve on what did not. Robert Tillberg made two trips on the *Canberra* to get a feel for the ship before he started his designs.

The P&O Chairman, Lord Sterling, had overall say on what was to be built and it was his insistence that the ship must have a graceful appearance

*The **Aurora** is seen here in her natural environment with cruise customers enjoying her ample outside deck space. (FotoFlite)*

The **Oriana**'s funnel is a single stack designed to
look like two in reverence to P&O's most famous
ship, the **Canberra**. She was also the last ship
built for P&O to have open bridge wings.
(FotoFlite)

with the raked stern so that she would look appealing to the British market. He also wanted a large promenade deck as this is something that British passengers had enjoyed since they first went to sea. There were technical requirements for the new ship in terms of speed, sea-keeping qualities, safety and a need for a shallower draught to increase the number of ports that the ship could visit. As she was to be designed for worldwide cruises, larger than normal fuel and water tanks would be required. Due to the constraints of the Panama Canal her hull could be no wider than 32.2 metres yet had to be stronger than usual as she would need to achieve a speed of 24 knots in all but the most extreme of weather.

DESIGN

When the first design was completed in September 1990, the project was put to 12 European shipyards, including the three British shipyards capable of building such a ship but it was clear that under the original design the ship was going to be too big and too expensive. None of the British yards were interested and only Meyer Werft in Germany and Kvaerner Masa yards in Finland could meet P&O's desired delivery date. These two shipyards were invited to re-tender and submit their own general arrangements for the ship based on P&O's requirements. Kvaerner came up with a ship which was too small for P&O's needs but Meyer Werft designed a ship of 260 metres in length, around 69,000 gross tons in size and one that would carry just over 1,700 passengers on ten decks. The P&O board realised that this was the ship for them. She was to be the largest ship ever built by Meyer Werft or ordered by P&O Cruises.

The contract was signed in December 1991 at a cost of £200 million and announced to the world in the following month. Agreements were made for a second ship to be considered if the markets warranted it. Being a British ship, P&O had invited many British companies to tender for work on the new vessel and contracts were signed with many British companies. This included Brintons of Kidderminster who were to provide the carpets, Earlys of Witney who provided the soft furnishings in the cabins and Ravenhead who provided the glassware for the bars and restaurants. Suppliers of the propellers, stabilisers and rudders were also to be British. The new ship would have 17 public rooms, more than on any other build at the time, and a greater range of cabin accommodation to appeal to all sections of the British cruise market. She would have the largest swimming pool ever built for a cruise ship and more outside deck space than anything else afloat. The *Canberra* theme was to be continued with open bridge wings with one funnel designed to look like two and angled stiffeners between the lifeboats. At the insistence of the ship's first Captain, Ian Gibb, a proper ship's wheel was fitted to the computerised bridge.

CONSTRUCTION

Before any construction of the *Oriana* could begin, two models of the design were made and tested in an experimental model tank in Trondheim, Norway. The models were tested in up to Force 10 conditions which allowed for the optimum design for the ship's hull that has the minimum resistance for the required speed. Sea keeping is a compromise between speed and stability and these tests allowed for the best design to be calculated for the required specification. Having finished the tank tests, the models were moved to Vienna for further aerodynamic tests in wind tunnels. Tests on model propellers and rudders were also carried out as well as studies into noise and vibration reduction. Almost a year after the contract was signed, the final design was approved and the first steel used to build the ship was cut. The first block of the *Oriana* was laid inside Meyer

The shopping complex on the **Oriana** *is set around her main atrium and is named Knightsbridge after one of London's most famous shopping districts. (John Hendy)*

Both ships have a bar named after one of P&O's co founders, Arthur Anderson. They were designed by John McNeece to have the feel of a London Gentleman's club. (John Hendy)

When she entered service in 1995, the **Oriana** *had more public rooms than any other cruise ship afloat. Here we see another of her show lounges where entertainment is provided every night. (John Hendy)*

*All successful British cruise ships have ample outside deck space. On the **Oriana** and the **Aurora** there are outside bars overlooking their sterns which become luxury grills at night. (John Hendy)*

*The Cricketers' Pub on the **Oriana** was another throwback to the **Canberra**. It proved to be so popular with passengers that it was increased in size during the ship's refit of 2006. (P&O Cruises)*

The Mini Suites on both ships bring true luxury and space at an affordable price. A huge private balcony with your own private sun loungers make the experience extra special.(P&O Cruises)

Werft's giant 370-metre long construction hall on 11th March 1993. The traditional lucky pennies were laid by the Chairman of P&O Cruises, Tim Harris and the managing director of the shipyard, Bernard Meyer. It was at this ceremony that the name *Oriana* was confirmed after Lord Sterling had chosen it over the other option, *Arcadia*.

The *Oriana* was built on the block principle using 45 prefabricated blocks. The largest of these was block 16 which at 722 tonnes would house the engines. The total amount of steel used in the *Oriana*'s construction was 14,444 tonnes. When designing the *Oriana*'s engineering spaces the technical team at P&O had gone for the traditional engine and gearbox arrangement rather than the more modern diesel electric arrangement which is found in all contemporary large passenger ships. This means she has eight diesel engines, four for propulsion and four for mains electricity. This arrangement does take up a lot of valuable space but means that the ship has a unique feel when she is in service as there is a certain vibration you experience with gearboxes that you don't with diesel electric machinery. The technical team had also elected to use shaft propellers and rudders and not the new and evolutionary Azipod pod propulsion system. Although Azipods do offer smoother running and greater manoeuvrability, they are very expensive to build and maintain and were an untested technology in 1995.

The *Oriana* has M.A.N diesel engines with the propulsion engines arranged in the father and son configuration with the smaller engines outside of the larger engines. The larger engines are 9-cylinder in line heavy marine oil engines with a total weight of 211 tonnes producing just under 12,000kW at 428rpm. The smaller engines are 6-cylinder of the same design weighing in at 149 tonnes and producing 7,950kW at the same speed. This gives a shaft power of 39,750kW (54,000HP). The four generators each provide 4,400kW of electrical power for all of the ship's electrical needs including the hotel, back of house and engineering requirements. To give some idea of scale, this is exactly the same as the total engine output of Brittany Ferries' ferry, *Normandie*. The two propellers are manufactured by the Dutch company L.I.P.S and made of Cunial, a mixture of copper, nickel and aluminium. Each weighs 32 tonnes and has four 5.8-metre wide blades. They are variable pitched which means the engines never go into reverse. The *Oriana* has three bow thrusters and one stern thruster to assist with manoeuvring. The whole propulsion system is operated by one joystick through the Lipstronic computerised control system. This single lever coordinates the propellers, thrusters and rudders in one operation.

ON BOARD

When British passengers go on board a ship they expect the ship to look like a ship and not a floating hotel. With this in mind Robert Tillberg adopted a more ship-like design in his drawings. For example in the cabins there were no sharp corners on the furniture. He also designed arches which are reminiscent of traditional ships. Wood was extensively used with laminates that looked like wood. The *Oriana* has more baths in the cabins than any other cruise ship. This is because the British like to have baths whilst most foreign passengers prefer a shower. Classic textile patterns have been used throughout the ship along with strong colours. None of the public rooms have polished metals, neon lights or any of the glitzy razzmatazz that you find on American-based cruise ships. The *Oriana* is a one-class ship, all of which is first class but, in an effort to please everyone, certain areas have been designed to appeal more to some passengers then others. The design brief was to have many smaller public rooms which

*The after staircase is seen here on the **Aurora**. Her carpets were provided by Brintons of Kidderminster while the artwork on the bulkheads was all specially commissioned for the ship. (Miles Cowsill)*

*On the **Aurora** John McNeece decided to give the ship an extra special feature; her own fireplace which is the only one of its kind on any cruise ship. (Miles Cowsill)*

*The Sportsbar on the **Aurora** is called Champions and is very popular with the ship's younger cruisers. Live sporting events are shown on multiple TV screens. (Miles Cowsill)*

appeal to the British public. At the time of the *Oriana*'s construction almost all new cruise ships were being designed for the North American market whose trend is to go for much larger rooms where large numbers of passengers can mix at the same time. This is why P&O ships have two main restaurants whilst American ships have one vast restaurant. American ships also have much bigger casinos, theatres and bars but a much smaller amount of outside deck space. The British public like to sunbathe when they are on holiday so British ships have much more open deck spaces than American ships. The *Oriana* also has a vast amount of British art on board. Paintings by artists including Janet Shearer and David Hiscock and sculptures by John Mills and James Butler fill the passenger spaces to combine with natural light and high-quality soft furnishings to really set the feel of British luxury. The ship even has its own London club named after one of P&O's founders, Arthur Anderson. Passengers could look forward to the largest spa ever built on a British ship, a theatre of such technical innovation it could put on shows seen in London's West End, a four storey Atrium that simply takes your breath away and more bars to enjoy themselves in than most small towns.

Construction of the *Oriana* continued until she was finally ready for out docking on 7th January 1995. Once out of the building hall, her funnel was added and the ship was all but complete. She left Papenburg a month later for her journey down the River Ems to the North Sea. Her sea trials were carried out in March 1995 where the wind did not drop below Force 7. Finally she was officially handed over to P&O on 2nd April 1995, sailing directly to Southampton where she arrived two days later. The ship was named on the 6th April by Her Majesty the Queen and commenced her Maiden Voyage to the Canary Islands on 9th April.

A SECOND SHIP

The *Oriana* was immediately a great success and numbers travelling with P&O increased significantly as the new ship generated her own trade. Everyone loved the ship and wanted to be among the first to travel on her. It was clear that the numbers of passengers wishing to travel from the UK were increasing and future predictions showed this would continue well into the 21st century. The P&O board were delighted with the public response to the ship and at a meeting in early 1997 it was agreed to order a second ship based on the success of the *Oriana* but to incorporate improvements where necessary.

It was immediately decided that the new ship should be bigger with more cabins and extra passenger facilities. The new design incorporated the same number of decks and a few minor changes to the public rooms. Lord Sterling chose the name *Aurora* as she was to be the first ship of the new Millennium and the Roman Goddess of Dawn seemed to be the perfect choice. The new ship would be 10 metres longer bringing her length up to 270 metres and her gross tonnage up to 76,512. The *Oriana* had 912 cabins, 118 of them with their own private balcony. Despite the additional cost of having a balcony it was clear that passengers were prepared to pay the extra for this little bit of private luxury. On every *Oriana* cruise the balcony cabins were the first grade to be sold out. The number of cabins on the new ship was to be enlarged to 939 with the number of balconied cabins dramatically increased to 406 cabins. A new level of luxury was to be added with two new multi-level penthouses at the front of the ship. They were to have private balconies on both decks, a bar area, luxury living area and a dining area for six people. With each suite offering around 865 square feet of space they really were to be the last word in luxury. With the *Oriana* starting her cruises in Britain, it was often two days into a cruise before

The **Aurora**'s main atrium features a 35 foot tall, Lalique style sculpture of two mythical figures behind a veil of water. Rising through four decks, it truly is the heart of the ship. (Miles Cowsill)

passengers could use the swimming pools. It was therefore decided that the *Aurora* would have a retractable roof over her main swimming pool so that this popular feature could be used in any weather. The Crow's Nest Lounge was moved directly over the navigation bridge so that passengers received an uninterrupted view out over the ship's bow.

On the engineering side the ship was completely re-designed. This time diesel electric was chosen as the preferred choice of propulsion although the *Aurora* would still have shafts and rudders rather than Azipod propulsion. Out went the father and son engine arrangement in favour of four V14 M.A.N heavy marine diesel engines. Each weighs 209 tonnes and produces 14,700kW of power giving the ship a total output of 58,800kW or 79,860HP. This is all turned into electricity, some of which is used for propulsion and the rest to power the ship. The propulsion is through two A.E.G 20,00kW electric motors which in turn power the shafts to the propellers. Unlike the *Oriana*, the *Aurora*'s propellers are fixed pitch as the electric motors control the speed and direction of the shaft. The blades are smaller than on the *Oriana* but this time there are five blades instead of four. The bridge was to be totally enclosed and there would be no ship's wheel; all control is via the ship's computer.

Meyer Werft were again chosen to build the ship and on 23rd April 1997 the contract was signed for a price close to that of the *Oriana*. However, this time more European companies tendered for work on the new ship although Robert Tillberg was again asked to design the ship's interior. Her keel was laid down on 15th December 1998. A total of 63 building blocks were used bringing the total amount of steel in the *Aurora*'s construction to 16,500 tonnes, just over 2,000 tonnes more than the *Oriana*. She was floated up on 7th August 1999 and finally floated out of the building hall on 8th January 2000. On 26th February, she was the last Meyer Werft cruise liner to go down the Ems bow first. All cruise ships built since the *Aurora* have been fitted with Azipod propulsion and pilots have found that by reversing a ship down the Ems they have better control as the ships have got bigger. The *Aurora*'s sea trials took place in the North Sea during March and she was finally handed over on 15th April 2000. She sailed directly to Southampton where she was named by Princess Anne on the 27th April. Unfortunately the champagne bottle failed to break against her hull and immediately some saw this as a bad omen. Regrettably they were proved to be right as just one day into her Maiden cruise, one of the white metal bearings on her portside propeller shaft overheated which required immediate attention. The ship returned to Southampton with all passengers given a full refund and a free cruise. The *Aurora* went back to Germany where the matter was rectified and was able to start her service with the next cruise to the Canary Islands.

The *Oriana* and *Aurora* are extremely well-designed and well-built ships. Today they are 16 and 11 years old respectively yet are in first-class condition. They are the two most popular ships in the P&O fleet with each having an extremely loyal band of passengers. As P&O Cruises is now part of the Carnival brand of companies, it is a realist fact that ships like these will never be built again. All new builds will be from a design which fits other Carnival brands such as Cunard or the Italian company, Costa Cruises. Such an example is the Vista class *Arcadia* which was fourth in a nine-ship build. This means that the *Oriana* and *Aurora* will be the last ever cruise ships designed from the outset as being exclusively for the British market. They are jewels amongst cruise ships with British pedigree, style and luxury which only P&O Cruises can provide.

*Many natural woods have been used throughout the two ships. Here in the **Aurora**'s library, passengers can enjoy plush carpets and comfortable seating to enhance their reading pleasure. (Miles Cowsill)*

The Aurora's Alexandra Restaurant has many features which have reference to Egypt. Large floor to ceiling windows give plenty of natural light and outstanding views. (Miles Cowsill)

Large teak decks are a feature of both ships' promenade decks which go right around the vessel. (Miles Cowsill)

The Riviera Pool on the **Aurora** is her large open air swimming pool. Her Crystal Pool has a retractable roof which can be closed when the weather is less favourable. (Miles Cowsill)

RIVIERA · POOL

Photo Feature-Hurtigruten

by John Bryant

3

The 'Hurtigruten' (literally the 'fast route' or 'coastal express' as it is known on board) is, with justification, referred to as the 'world's most beautiful sea voyage'. The journey from Bergen to Kirkenes and back is an unforgettable trip calling at 34 ports northbound and 33 ports southbound and covers a distance of over 2 500 miles in eleven days. Over half of the journey lies north of the Arctic Circle and it runs along a coastline which has no equal in Europe. In doing so you pass the westernmost point of Norway (just outside Sognefjord), almost the northernmost (North Cape, which you can visit) and the most easterly at Vardo (where you are actually east of Istanbul).

It is only when you actually make this trip that you begin to understand just how important this service is to the population who live in the most northern parts of Norway and the enterprise, experience and seamanship that was necessary to establish this link and maintain it. The esteem in which the Hurtigruten is held was ably demonstrated in June 2011 when the Norwegian Broadcasting Company, NRK, transmitted live all 134 hours of the *Nordnorge*'s northbound journey from Bergen to Kirkenes. Not only was this watched by millions around the world but thousands of Norwegians turned out to greet the ship at each port of call. The voyage ended with Queen Sonia welcoming the ship at Kirkenes from on board the Royal Yacht *Norge*.

There have been no less than nine companies involved since the route's inception in 1893 by Richard With's shipping company, Vesteraalens Dampskibsselskab. By 1996 it had been pared down to OVDS (Ofotens and Vesteraalens Dampskibsselskab) and TFDS (Troms Fylkes Dampskibsselskab) and in 2006 everything came under the umbrella of Hurtigruten ASA resulting in various minor livery changes as seen in the accompanying photographs taken between 2006 and 2011.

Currently there are 13 ships in the fleet; the two 'traditional' vessels *Nordstjernen* (1956) and *Lofoten* (1964) continue to be in excellent condition and both now have government 'heritage ship' status. The rather boxy *Vesteralen* (1983) is the last of the 'mid generation' vessels operating, modernised in both the late 80s and 90s and is comfortably functional. All three attract a niche following.

The six 'new generation' ships (*Kong Harald*, *Nordnorge*, *Nordkapp*, *Richard With*, *Nordlys*, and *Polarlys*) set new standards in the cruise element of the service when introduced between 1993 and 1997. They are all similar in design and layout but their interior decoration has been individually styled to reflect their name.

Of the three 'millennium' ships, the *Finnmarken* (2002) is an enlarged and further improved version of her six predecessors. Until October 2011 she was engaged on a lucrative charter to the oil and gas industry off north-west Australia, sporting an all white livery. Once the *Finnmarken* returns, this will see the retirement of the *Nordstjernen*. The sister ships *Trollfjord* (2002) and *Midnatsol* (2003) are different in style, luxuriously appointed and centred around a stunning atrium.

Hurtigruten's newest vessel is the *Fram* (2007), in essence she is a compact version of the *Finnmarken* but especially designed for explorer voyages around Antarctica (in winter) and Greenland (in summer).

With Hurtigruten ASA being re-awarded the contract to run the service until 2020, this has brought a fresh impetus to the company, particularly as the new government subsidy will enable an 11-ship daily service to operate throughout the year. In addition, at least one new vessel will be ordered and, once the *Finnmarken* returns, this will see the retirement of the *Nordstjernen*.

The only 'mid generation' vessel left in Hurtigruten service, the **Vesteralen** *(1983, 6,261 gross tons) was given a major rebuild in 1988 when her original container deck was replaced by a new accommodation block. Rather boxy in appearance with a large aft sun deck, internally her lounges are very comfortable and cosy. She is pictured off Havoysund in February 2009, southbound with Hammerfest as her next port of call. (John Bryant)*

*The exploration ship **Fram** (11,647 gross tons, built 2007 by Fincantieri, Italy) is designed to cope with all but the harshest ice conditions. Named after Nansen's famous ship ('fram' means forward), in summer she is based around Greenland and in the winter travels to Antarctica. She is seen here at Tower Bridge, London in April 2009 on a re-positioning cruise as she returned from the Southern Hemisphere. (John Bryant)*

*The first of what became the 'new generation' ships, the **Kong Harald** (1993, 11,204 gross tons) represented a new era in the Hurtigruten fleet. Commissioned by TFDS she is seen in their funnel colours close to Havøysund (Finnmark) as she journeys south to Hammerfest in May 2006. (John Bryant)*

The **Midnatsol** (16,151 gross tons) was completed at the Rissa Yard (near Trondheim) in 2003. With her two-level observation lounge and stunning interiors she is always well patronised. Used as an accommodation vessel for the 2004 Winter Olympics in Torino, the vessel has also visited both Portsmouth and the Pool of London. She is pictured at Trondheim in May 2006 still sporting her original TFDS funnel livery, whilst (below), she is in the current Hurtigruten livery as she powers past the forbidding 'Lofoten Wall' on her way to Stamsund from Solvaer in May 2011. (John Bryant)

Named after the most northerly point of mainland Norway, the **Nordkapp** (1996, 11,386 gross tons) seen approaching Trondheim on her northbound service to Kirkenes in June 2011. Built at Ulsteinvik for OVDS she was an improved version of her earlier three near sisters. The plethora of satellite navigation equipment on the top deck arises from her service in the Antarctic during our winter months from 2005 to 2007. (John Bryant)

South of Bodo and close to re-crossing the Arctic Circle, the **Lofoten** (2,621 gross tons) is well loved by a loyal and discerning clientele. The ship built by Aker, Oslo in 1964, is beautifully maintained and is once more permanently on the coastal steamer service. In 2000 she was given heritage status by the Riksantikvaren, Norway's Directorate for Cultural Heritage. (John Bryant)

In this view of the **Nordlys** *(1994, 11,204 gross tons) at Honningsvag (the port for the North Cape) in June 2011, the unique loading arrangements for the Hurtigruten fleet can be clearly seen. She is the only Hurtigruten ship to have moored at both Tyne Bridge, Newcastle and Tower Bridge, London. Laid up in late 2008, she soon returned to service deputising for the* **Richard With**. *She suffered a serious engine room fire approaching Alesund in September 2011. (John Bryant)*

The **Trollfjord** *(2002, 16,140 gross tons) marked a departure in design for the Hurtigruten, with lavish cool blue interiors centred on an atrium five decks high. Her hull was constructed at the Bruce Shipyard, Landskrona, Sweden, before being towed to the Rissa Yard, near Trondheim for completion. She is seen here in May 2011 departing Trondheim on her way south to Bergen. (John Bryant)*

Between 2002 and 2008 the **Nordnorge** (1997, 11,350 gross tons) spent her winters cruising in Antarctic waters. In the news in November 2007 when rescuing passengers from the sinking cruise ship **Explorer**, she spent 2008 as an accommodation vessel in the Adriatic but has since returned to full service on the Hurtigruten. In this June 2011 view she is seen arriving at Molde with the beautiful Romsdal Alps as the backdrop. (John Bryant)

The **Polarlys** (1996, 11,431 gross tons) is often referred to as the 'ship with a soul', her stunning interior lighting enhanced by large angled windows which capture the natural light. Built at Ulsteinvik for TFDS she is viewed in February 2008 at Alesund, from the summit of Mount Aksla (only 418 steps up!). The town itself was largely destroyed by fire in 1904 and rebuilt in Art Nouveau style, the famous Geiranger Fjord is close by. (John Bryant)

Poetry in motion, the **Nordstjernen** (1956, 2,191 gross tons) was built in Germany by Blohm & Voss and spent 38 years on the coastal express until 1994, when she was used on cruises to Svalbard and Greenland. Today she is back where she started, lovingly cared for and now listed as an historic ship by Norway's Directorate of Cultural Heritage. In the upper picture she is seen serenely departing from Trondheim in February 2008 whilst in the lower view she is getting underway from Molde, the 'town of roses', on her way south to Bergen in May 2011. To be withdrawn in Spring 2012. (John Bryant)

The **Finnmarken** (2002, 15,530 gross tons) was built at Ulsteinvik, south of Trondheim and is an upgraded version of her predecessors, more spacious, boasting many recreational facilities including a heated outdoor swimming pool. She is pictured (above) in her more usual snowy element at Sortland (Vesteraalen) in March 2009. Recently on charter as an accommodation ship in connection with the Gorgon oil and gas field off Barrow Island, north-west Australia. In the lower picture, taken in December 2009 she is seen being prepared for that role at Westcon's Olensvag Yard, Western Norway, with an all-white livery more suited to the tropical climate in which she was to operate. (John Bryant/Westcon)

*Named after the founder of the route, the **Richard With** (1993, 11,205 gross tons) was the first Hurtigruten ship to visit the Geiranger Fjord as part of its summer itinerary. The ship is pictured (above) in her OVDS funnel livery arriving at Harstad in May 2006. The ship is pictured in her OVDS funnel livery departing Rorvik in May 2006. Note the Hurtigruten tradition of waving towels and making as much noise as possible whenever Hurtigruten fleetmates pass each other .(John Bryant)*

*The **Finnmarken** (1956, 2,189 gross tons) built by Blohm & Voss (Germany) sailed on the coastal route until 1993. She was taken out of the water in 1999 to become an integral part of the new Hurtigruten Museum at Stockmarknes, Vesteraalen. The ship is Norway's largest land museum exhibit. The roof sheeting is an attempt to limit moisture damage in the winter but now appears to be a permanent feature. (John Bryant)*

4 MacBrayne's Islay Car Ferries

by Ian Hall

In 1964 David MacBrayne Limited introduced their first trio of purpose-built car ferries. However, Islay was not included in the original car ferry plan, and despite growing vehicle traffic, had to persevere with the 1939 crane-loading mailboat *Lochiel* sailing from the space restricted pier at West Loch Tarbert (WLT). The announcement of plans to build a 'holiday village' on the island led to increased pressure for a car ferry service and a meeting was held to discuss the possibility of a MacBrayne car ferry service from a new pier near the mouth of the West Loch.

EARLY DAYS

In 1965 MacBrayne's held public meetings on Islay, Jura, Gigha and Colonsay to gauge public opinion on a car ferry service. In the meantime, as a short-term measure to provide additional capacity, the Oban-based mailboat *Lochnevis* (1934) took over the Islay mail roster in July and August, freeing the *Lochiel* to provide a supplementary twice-daily service between WLT and Port Askaig (Islay), primarily for car traffic. In the following summers, this arrangement operated at weekends only.

By 1966, MacBraynes and Argyll County Council had agreed on a plan for a drive-on drive-off ferry to serve Port Askaig, Port Ellen (Islay) and Colonsay from a new council-built terminal at Redhouse, near the mouth of the West Loch. However, opposition to this plan from supporters of the 'Overland Route', which entailed short crossings from the mainland to Jura and from Jura to Port Askaig, resulted in much debate and delay.

Whilst the arguments raged, in April 1968, a private operator, Western Ferries, rather stole MacBrayne's thunder by introducing a stern loading ro-ro ferry, the *Sound of Islay* on a service between Kennacraig, further down the West Loch from MacBrayne's pier, and Port Askaig. This service prospered and was particularly favoured by the lucrative commercial traffic serving the whisky distilleries. By the following year a connectional service between Port Askaig and Feolin (Jura) had been introduced and a larger drive-through ferry, *Sound of Jura*, was placed on the service to the mainland.

In 1968 the Secretary of State ruled in favour of a large ferry to serve Islay and Colonsay from Redhouse, with Jura and Gigha served by small ferries on short crossings. The 'Overland Route' was rejected on the grounds of cost. Despite the arrival of competition, MacBrayne pressed on

*A busy scene at Port Askaig, as the **Glen Sannox** makes her afternoon call. February 1981. The ship became a regular visitor to Islay in a relief or emergency role until her withdrawal in 1989. The fast and spacious ship became a great favourite amongst the islanders. (Ian Hall)*

The **Claymore** at Port Ellen. March 1997. Entering service in 1978, her slower service speed meant an extension to the advertised crossing times. Her final crossings for CalMac were in 1997 although she subsequently appeared under new ownership. (Ian Hall)

The **Pioneer** alongside West Loch Tarbert Pier. April 1977. Entering service in 1974, the Leith-built ship was always fast on passage and was able to accommodate more artics than her fleet companions. Following the removal of the mainland terminal to Kennacraig in 1978, she frequently made the crossing in 1 hour 45 minutes. (Ian Hall)

as best they could with their own plans. In December they placed an order with the Ailsa yard at Troon for an £840,000 drive-through ferry, which would also have a side-loading hoist, for use at Colonsay.

MacBrayne's joy at this progress was short-lived as in January 1969, Argyll County Council decided that they would not, after all, proceed with the £250,000 terminal at Redhouse. After further debate and the intervention of the Scottish Office, a compromise solution was reached in April for a cheaper terminal (£100,000) further up the loch at Escart Bay. However, nothing further was heard of this scheme and in August, the Scottish Transport Group, new owners of both MacBrayne and the Caledonian Steam Packet Company, announced that the Islay issue would be solved in the short term by the simple expedient of transferring the CSP's pioneer hoist loading Clyde car ferry *Arran* (1953) to the Islay service before the end of the year. This vessel was capable of using the existing pier at WLT. The new custom-built Islay ferry would provide much needed extra vehicle capacity on the Clyde.

ARRAN

Stunned by this turn of events with regard to both ships and terminals, MacBraynes had no option but to make the best of what they had, and on 19th January 1970, the *Arran* entered service on the traditional Islay roster, serving Port Ellen and Port Askaig, as well as Gigha, Craighouse on Jura and Colonsay. The 16-year-old ferry had undergone a £40,000 refit for her new duties. A connecting parcels and freight service by lorry was also introduced and as a result both the *Lochiel* and the cargo vessel *Loch Ard* (1955), which sailed from Glasgow to Islay, were withdrawn. The *Arran* allowed MacBraynes to compete to some extent for vehicle traffic, but maintaining the service when the side loader was off for annual overhaul was a problem as the other MacBrayne car ferries couldn't use WLT. As a result of this, when the *Clansman* (1964) relieved the *Arran* in March 1971 she had to run between Oban and Port Askaig. In April of the following year, the ship which should have been serving Islay, the *Iona* (1970) filled this role.

The company's woes were far from over, as in November 1971 the Scottish Secretary announced that MacBrayne's subsidy for the Islay route would be withdrawn at the end of March the following year and henceforth Western Ferries would be the sole operators on the route. MacBraynes duly announced their withdrawal from the route and planned to redeploy the *Arran* as second boat on the Dunoon crossing. However, Islay didn't want a private monopoly any more than they wanted a state monopoly and there was considerable opposition to this plan. An inquiry found against the proposal and the MacBrayne service was firstly extended to 30th September and later indefinitely. Around this time, Western Ferries approached STG with a view to selling out but this fell through and in December it was revealed that the *Arran* would be withdrawn from service at the end of the year for conversion to ro-ro operation.

At the Barclay Curle yard in Glasgow, the *Arran* was stripped of her hoist and all superstructure at the after end, creating an open car deck capable of carrying articulated lorries. She was fitted with a stern ramp and the piers at WLT and Port Ellen received basic alterations to suit ro-ro operations. In her new guise she was briefly tried out on the Arran run before she returned to the fray at Islay on 19th April 1973. She gave three return sailings between WLT and Port Ellen only and sailed in the colours of Caledonian MacBrayne, following the amalgamation of the two STG shipping companies. This relatively inexpensive conversion enabled MacBrayne to better compete with Western Ferries, but the removal of all

The **Arran** in ro-ro condition berths at West Loch Tarbert Pier. February 1975. Dating from 1953, the **Arran** was transferred to Islay in 1970 and facilitated the handling of additional vehicle traffic. Her introduction allowed the traditional cargo services from Glasgow to be withdrawn. (Graeme Dunlop)

The chartered **Claymore** at Port Askaig in Argyll & Antrim Steam Packet Co. colours. March 1998. The former CalMac ship deputised on the Islay link between 1997 and 1999. (Ian Hall)

The chartered **Pentalina B** arriving at Port Askaig. April 2009. Serving in primarily a freight role, the former CalMac favourite **Iona** was hastily chartered from her new Orkney-based owners in April 2009 following a breakdown to the **Isle of Arran**. (Ian Hall)

weight aft meant that her screws sat rather high in the water, and resulted in propeller cavitations when the engines were put astern. Henceforth she could be difficult to handle when manoeuvring at the piers.

A PURPOSE-BUILT SHIP

A more permanent solution was in sight from February 1973, when the STG ordered a £1 million new building for the Islay route from the Robb Caledon shipyard in Leith. This vessel was named *Pioneer* at her launch in April 1974 and was ready for service by mid-August. Although she did not bring a huge increase in capacity over her predecessor, the *Pioneer* could carry more artics, was faster, was equipped with all the latest navigational aids, and her two passenger lounges were bright, modern and comfortable. Cranes were also fitted to enable her to handle vehicles and cargo on her calls at Gigha. The *Pioneer* also had that indefinable charisma that a select few ferries possess, and became a great favourite throughout her career with CalMac. Few who saw her speeding down the West Loch with a perfect bow wave, forgot the sight. The *Arran* became spare but she still returned to Islay to relieve the newcomer for annual overhaul.

The original idea was that CalMac's fleet of modern car ferries would be able to operate without subsidy, but this proved to be a forlorn hope and as early as 1976, the Islay route was losing £247,000 per annum. In August of that year traffic was boosted markedly after Western Ferries sold the *Sound of Jura* and the smaller *Sound of Islay* returned to their Islay service. This was the beginning of the end for the private company and in 1981 they pulled off the route.

From 26th June 1978, the *Pioneer* started using the mainland terminal at Kennacraig, which CalMac had taken over. Now, with a shorter passage to the open sea, she was sometimes able to make the crossing to Islay in just 1 hour 45 minutes instead of the advertised 2 hours.

With ever-growing traffic a larger vessel was now needed, and the arrival of new tonnage at Oban meant that in February 1979 the *Iona* could at last take up the route for which she was built, replacing the *Pioneer*. The *Iona* was too large to call at Gigha, so the *Bruernish* served that island from Kennacraig, until the completion of a new terminal at Tayinloan. CalMac served both Islay ports from October that year, when the *Iona* re-introduced calls at Port Askaig pier. When she took up service at Islay, the *Iona* had already earned a reputation for versatility, good handling characteristics and being an excellent sea boat, and she proved to be a boon to the route. One drawback was that raising her bow visor was a somewhat cumbersome procedure, and so with a busy schedule, she tended to operate as a stern loader.

At first the *Pioneer* returned as overhaul relief, but by now she was becoming too small even for the winter traffic. In January 1981, the *Glen Sannox* (1957) made the first of many appearances on the Islay service as relief or in emergency. She had been extensively reconditioned and re-engined in 1977, her commodious passenger accommodation proved popular with travellers and she was also fast and powerful. Compared to more modern ferries however, she had neither direct bridge control of the engines, nor controllable pitch propellers, so she required a bit more 'notice' of impending manoeuvres. While a linkspan was installed at Kennacraig in 1989, the *Glen Sannox* ran between Port Askaig and Oban, and in May of the same year, she inaugurated a new summer Wednesday timetable, which featured a through return sailing on the routing Kennacraig-Port Askaig-Colonsay-Oban. This proved very popular with tourists. The *Glen Sannox* made her last sailings on the Islay run in June 1989, shortly before her final withdrawal from the fleet.

ENTER THE CLAYMORE

Once again, the arrival of new tonnage at Oban resulted in a change of ship for Islay in June 1989. Now the stern-loading *Claymore* (1978) was allocated to the service, with timings eased to suit her slower speed. Her interior passenger areas were refurbished in a pleasing style and she became a reliable performer on the run. The *Iona* still appeared each winter as relief vessel.

Cascaded tonnage was now the norm for Islay, and the next reshuffle took place in 1993, following the introduction of a new Arran ferry. A new linkspan had been provided at Kennacraig in June, during which time a temporary service to Oban was operated by the *Claymore* and *Pioneer*, and the new vessel, the *Isle of Arran* (1984), appeared on the run in August. She was a much larger ship than hitherto employed, and brought more space for cars and commercials. The latter was especially important for Islay's successful distillery trade, which generated considerable two-way lorry traffic. The *Isle of Arran* also had good open deck space, a quiet/no smoking lounge; a disabled lift from car deck to the accommodation and for those on the bridge, Becker rudders gave increased agility at piers. She was also drive through and bow loaded at Kennacraig and stern loaded at island ports. The Illeachs didn't have much time to get used to their new ship though, as the *Isle of Arran* was to be fleet relief vessel in winter and was away from October until Christmas standing in on various other routes. After ten years of working on the busy Arran run, her passenger lounges were in need of refurbishment, and this was done early in 1994.

It was also in 1994 that the Mull ferry *Isle of Mull* (1988) made her one and only visit to date to Islay when she sailed in emergency from Oban to Port Askaig.

The *Claymore*'s last duties under CalMac ownership were as relief to the *Isle of Arran* at Islay in April 1997. The Leith-built vessel was the subject of an enforced sale to SeaCo. for the new seasonal Campbeltown to Ballycastle service. It wasn't long before she was back on familiar ground though, as the sale agreement allowed for her to be bareboat chartered to CalMac for the winter of 97/98. She served Islay from the end of October until March, now sporting the blue hull of the Argyll & Antrim Steam Packet Co. and having had a further upgrading of her passenger areas. The *Claymore* had three further spells covering at Islay in November 1998, February and April 1999.

From winter 1998, the *Isle of Arran* was at Islay year round. She was relieved for refit by the *Lord of the Isles* (1989) in March 1999, the first time the then Mallaig-based vessel had been used on the Islay service. A year later the *Hebridean Isles* (1985) was the relief vessel, a useful rehearsal as this ferry replaced her quasi-sister *Isle of Arran* on the route in March 2001. Displaced from the Uig triangle, she brought a better layout and a higher standard of passenger accommodation than her sister. The older ship returned from the end of August 2002 until April 2003, while the *Hebridean Isles* was standing in at Orkney for associated company NorthLink. The *Hebridean Isles* subsequently relieved at Orkney in February each year until 2007.

The spare *Isle of Arran* made additional sailings on the Islay route in the summer of 2003, mainly as a result of increased distillery freight, and, in the light of recent experience at Stornoway, to reduce the threat of an interloper coming in to cream off this traffic. By 2005 she found herself increasingly making extra freight runs outwith the summer period (sometimes on reduced crewing with a passenger certificate for 84) and by October 2007 she was usually on station at Islay as part of a two-ship

Clyde ferry **Saturn** *makes her unique call at Port Ellen on 15th September 2007. Built in 1977, the Clyde-based ship was in the process of testing both island ramps in case she was ever required in an emergency.(Iain McPherson)*

An aerial view of the **Lord of the Isles** *at Port Askaig. March 1999. Built ten years earlier, this was the first occasion that the then Mallaig-based vessel had serviced the Islay routes. (Ian Hall)*

*The **Isle of Arran** (1984) first appeared on the Islay route in 1993 and was particularly successful, her larger vehicle deck making her ideal for the carriage of freight which absorbed the considerable distillery traffic from the island. (Stuart MacKillop)*

*Replaced on the Uig triangle route, the **Hebridean Isles** first appeared at Islay for relief cover during early 2000. Her spacious accommodation was greatly appreciated by the islanders and she replaced the 'Arran' in March 2001. (Miles Cowsill)*

*The £24.5 million **Finlaggan** entered service on the Islay link during June 2011. The Polish-built vessel provides Islay with a purpose-built ship bringing both extra capacity and high levels of comfort to the island she serves. For the first time, laterally opening clamshell bow doors have been employed rather than an up-and-over visor. (Stuart MacKillop)*

service all year round. In 2009 both regular Islay vessels were fitted with 'Coffee Cabin' outlets in their former bars.

There have been two other notable visitors to the route in recent years. In September 2007, the estuarial ferry *Saturn* (1977) left the Clyde for the first time and conducted trials at Kennacraig and both island ports, to gauge her suitability for use as a freighter in emergency. From 1st to 17th April 2009, following an accident to *Isle of Arran*, the *Pentalina B* was chartered from Pentland Ferries, and supported the *Hebridean Isles*, largely in a freight capacity. Remarkably this was none other than the former *Iona*, which had been sold to Orkney in 1997.

The latest phase of the story commenced in 2002 when CalMac consulted stakeholders on the future shape of services to Islay. In 2004 they announced plans to build a new ferry for the route, together with associated major pier works at Kennacraig and Port Ellen (a major re-build

of Port Askaig was already underway). Late in 2007 Caledonian Maritime Assets Ltd who were now the owners of tonnage and terminals, placed a £24.5 million order for the new ferry with Remontowa of Poland. On 30th June 2010, the new vessel was launched at Gdansk and named *Finlaggan*. She entered service on Wednesday 1st June 2011.

The *Finlaggan*, based on the design of *Hamnavoe*, brings additional capacity to the route, and shorter journey times, together with a new level of comfort in her four passenger lounges. She is also the first CalMac vessel to have clamshell bow doors, instead of the more usual lifting visor. The arrival of this fine vessel marks the start of a new era in the continuing story of sea travel to Islay.

THE DEVELOPMENT OF ISLAY'S CAR FERRIES

NAME	BUILT	LENGTH (METRES)	GROSS TONNAGE	SPEED (KNOTS)	PASSENGERS*	VEHICLES *
Arran	1953	54.5	540	14	272	22 cars or 3 artics +15 cars
Pioneer	1974	67.0	1071	16	273	32 cars or 6 artics + 10 cars
Iona	1970	74.3	1324	15.5	524	47 cars or 11 artics + 7 cars
Claymore	1978	77.1	1631	14	500	53 cars or 6 artics + 23 cars
Isle of Arran	1984	84.9	3296	15	659	62 cars or 10 artics
Hebridean Isles	1985	85.2	3040	15	494	62 cars or 10 artics
Finlaggan	2011	89.8	5209	16.3	550	85 or 10 artics

* Passenger & Car capacity is current. Artics at yr of build.

5 A Purser at Sea

by Darren Holdaway

A phone call at 14.00 on 11th April 1991 was the start of a new career and an exciting new challenge. The call was from Sealink Stena's Southampton office inviting me for an interview with Hotel Manager Edgar King to join the newly formed route to Cherbourg which was operated by the ex Harwich-Hook giant, *Stena Normandy*.

The following weekend I joined the ship for my first time at sea before initially starting scheduled weekends followed by a permanent week on, week off rota. All was good for four years until the sad demise of such an interesting and exciting period to my life when the route sadly closed. I was then sent to Harwich to end the traditional Harwich-Hook route with the *Stena Europe*. I left the ship in the Hook and sailed back in the *Koningin Beatrix*.

Following a short break after leaving the Harwich operations, in February 1997 I was approached by Seamariner, a shipping agency based in Hythe, near Southampton, who asked me to join the ever popular *Sally Sky* which was in refit in dry dock, just outside the port of Vlissingen in the Netherlands. I duly obliged and was asked to join the ship the following day.

I made my way up to Ramsgate and was met by a Sally Line representative who put me on the late morning Jetfoil service to Ostend. On arrival I was greeted by a taxi and driven to Vlissingen where I joined the ship in a very cold and foggy dry dock during the early evening. My time on board the *Sally Sky* was both enjoyable and hospitable with only a skeleton crew of 12 on board. A few weeks were spent in the dry dock before we sailed back to Ramsgate where we made two or three round trips in a freight-only mode to Ostend, before moving again, to Tilbury.

During our period in Tilbury, the *Sally Sky* was transformed into Holyman Sally's *Eurotraveller* which during this period had the 'cow catcher' fixed to her bow and a rebranding and repainting in Holyman Sally's livery. Three months were spent on this vessel looking after the officer cabins, cooking breakfast (on one occasion) with some time spent in the pot wash and preparing the Officers' Mess for meals combined with general housekeeping of the officer areas. My time on *Eurotraveller* soon came to end and I disembarked from the vessel in Ostend.

It was time to move on with a couple of stopgap temporary positions with Red Funnel and Wightlink followed by another four great years at Portsmouth. The *Pride of Portsmouth* was waiting for me after a quick

*The **St. Faith** outward from Portsmouth to Fishbourne in September 1994. The vessel remains in service today with three of her sisters and the Polish-built **St. Clare**. (Miles Cowsill)*

The **Stena Normandy** was built in Gothenburg, Sweden in 1982 as the **Prinsessan Birgitta** and was designed for the Gothenburg-Frederikshavn route. She later became the **St Nicholas** and operated the Harwich-Hook of Holland route until 1981 when she transferred to the newly formed Southampton-Cherbourg service when she was in turn re-named **Stena Normandy**. She is seen here outbound from Southampton in the summer of 1996. (Andrew Cooke)

Built in 1975 at the Aalborg yard in Denmark as the **Viking Venturer**. She was renamed **Pride of Hampshire** in 1989 whilst serving the Portsmouth-Le Havre route but was later transferred to the Cherbourg route after the entry into service of the former Olau twins. After the closure of the Portsmouth services she moved south to the Mediterranean and was later re-named **Oujda** for Comanav on their Sete-Nador service. She is seen arriving at Portsmouth during November 1997. (Andrew Cooke)

Built in Bremerhaven, Germany, as the **Olau Britannia** in 1990 the ship operated with Olau until 1994, when she was chartered to P&O Ferries (Portsmouth) and became the **Pride of Portsmouth**. She operated the route between Portsmouth and Le Havre until P&O ceased operations. She currently operates for Italian operator SNAV as the **SNAV Lazio** between Naples and Palermo. (Darren Holdaway)

interview in Eastleigh at the Quest agency, which at this time were recruiting for P&O Portsmouth vessels. So it was off to Le Havre on the afternoon sailing, my cabin a nice single outside with shared bathroom for the crew below the main reception area.

Depending on operational requirements it is sometimes necessary to move crew around different vessels, this is usually the case to cover sickness, no show, resignations and so on and it was not long before I found myself covering the *Pride of Hampshire* on a temporary basis. She had so much to offer, the whole atmosphere and ambiance within the crew was fascinating. A great bonding, a friendly altogetherness which made the ship feel special and which had a positive effect on our work. They say, happy crew, happy ship, and she surely was; she had such a great character within herself, which made her very popular with her crew. However, with P&O Portsmouth at an end, it was time to look further afield, and this is where I am today.

Whether it was the *Stena Normandy*, *Pride of Hampshire*, *Pride of Portsmouth*, *St Faith* or *Red Eagle*, I could be directing passengers from the car deck to passenger areas, serving breakfast on the *Pride of Hampshire* or selling cabins or preparing accommodation or public spaces on the *Pride of Portsmouth*. Making cabins, serving in the bar on a Friday and Saturday night booze cruise on board the *Stena Normandy* (which was always fun, to say the least) it was all too often that foul language came from the passenger side of the bar! Behind the scenes, the 'Normandy' was also another great favourite of mine with a great crew and much fun to work and play on. Other jobs at this time involved selling coffee/tea or a simple postcard and cleaning tables or vacuuming the passenger spaces on Wightlink's *St Faith*, issuing vomit bags on a regular sea-sick run to Jersey on the *Varangerfjord* with Channel Hoppers, never knowing if we were going to return the same day or not. This in some cases was predictable but an overnight in a comfortable hotel in Jersey certainly was popular with the crew.

Life on board the Isle of Wight ships was simple but also a pleasure. There were many great people but not knowing which side of the Solent you are on at any given time of the day can be quite puzzling. I frequently imagined that I was in Portsmouth or Southampton and on looking out of the porthole found that we were actually in Fishbourne or Cowes! So many times a day back and forth can be a little confusing.

After six exciting and fun-filled years on board the ferries of Sealink (Stena) P&O, Wightlink and Red Funnel I felt it was time for a change. I was eagerly watching cruise ships coming and going in my home town and port of Southampton, so I was determined to try to further my knowledge and experience. Not only that but I felt that after going back and forth to the ports of Cherbourg and Le Havre, there was more out there in the world to offer, and so in January 1997, I decided to reply to an advertisement in the local 'Southampton Evening Echo'.

DEEP SEA

With the interview selection for Princess Cruises at the Dolphin Hotel in Southampton completed, there followed a short wait to see if it was all the start of something new; a new adventure, a new career. A letter came through the post a few days later together with a flight ticket to join the *Crown Princess*, now part of P&O's Australia fleet.

For the first three weeks life was full of familiarisation, training and learning about the company policies and procedures as well as the United States public health and Coastguard drills. This was followed by an assignment to join the *Regal Princess* in Acapulco, Mexico, where I would spend the next six months in my floating home cruising between Acapulco

The **Celebrity Constellation** was built by Chantiers d'Atlantique in Brest in 2001 and currently operates for Celebrity Cruises on a wide range of European/US and worldwide itineraries. During 2010 she was refurbished to Solstice class standards so that her amenities on board are similar to those of her larger fleet sisters. She is seen here in the picturesque port of Bonaire in the Caribbean. (Darren Holdaway)

The **Disney Magic** is seen approaching St Maarten in the Caribbean during February 2011. She was built in 1998 at the Fincantieri shipyard in Italy. (Darren Holdaway)

and Fort Lauderdale in Florida. There I met many exciting people, mixed nationalities and cultures, not only the passengers, but also the many crew members who made the ship feel like one big family.

It was not long before the Princess flag fell under the Carnival brand and this brought many changes, some for the good, some not so good. It followed that old ships began to leave the fleet and were replaced by larger ships, which seems to be the norm in this day and age. However, whether sailing the Mexican Riviera or Panama Canal, taking a ship trans-Atlantic, cruising the beauty of the Mediterranean or facing the challenging waters of the South China Sea, it's all been part of my life and job working on these beautiful ships, and visiting ports around the world to which I have been fortunate and thankful to sail. I could find myself on the smallest ship in the fleet or the most recent and largest ship sailing the seas today. As time has gone on and years passed, I have served on many ships in the Princess fleet and most currently where I am today, the Celebrity fleet.

From the 'Crown' and *Regal Princess* to the *Sky Princess* I moved to the 'Grand', 'Star', 'Golden', 'Diamond', 'Sapphire' and the current *Crown Princess*. My duties were to ensure a smooth and trouble-free arrival and departure of these ships into port, dealing with many challenges that may arise from local authorities, including immigration, customs and port agencies wanting anything from an extra guest manifest or to see a passenger who has been randomly selected from the manifest, to postcards or a t-shirt as a simple souvenir of their visit to the ship.

The *Pacific Sun* was being transformed from the *Carnival Jubilee* in the Bahamas shipyard in Freeport and I was asked to take her down to Sydney once the refit and P&O Australia logo and livery were completed. Delivery to her new owners in Sydney was temporarily delayed due to a hurricane that had hit the Bahamas. Damage was caused to the ship and crew members were put in local hotels until the ship was repaired.

Returning to the ship was quite amusing. I got to my cabin and found there was a gaping five-metre hole in the hull beside it. Welding and repair works went on for days and I remember stepping out of my bed the following morning into a foot of water which flooded my cabin and the others around it. An interesting but fun situation and a lot of tiring hard work ensued to prepare the ship ready for her departure a few days later to Australia. With all those sea days ahead, there would be a quick fuel stop in Cristobal, Panama, before moving on through the fascinating Panama Canal and onwards to Sydney, Australia.

Ten years with Princess Cruises was enough and it was time for a change for the better. I believed that standards were fast going downhill, especially after the Carnival merger which I strongly believe had a major effect on the whole Princess product. From my first ship, the *Crown Princess* I had moved to the 'Regal' as a Cabin Steward, then the 'Sun', 'Dawn', 'Ocean' and later the 'Diamond', 'Sapphire', 'Crown' and *Star Princess* as an Administration Purser and Front Desk Supervisor. The time had now come to move on and it was time to broaden my horizons.

ROYAL CARIBBEAN

It was time for a change; application forms were sent and interviews carried out for other companies. It was not long before replies started to return thick and fast and after careful consideration, it was Royal Caribbean Cruise Lines (RCCL) that looked the most appealing, and on one early Tuesday morning, my journey started to Addlestone in Surrey, the headquarters of Royal Caribbean.

The interview process was quick and I was hired on the Celebrity Cruises brand, taking into account my experience with the product and the

The **Norwegian Epic** was built by STX France in 2010 and can carry up to 4,200 passengers making her one of the largest cruise ships afloat today. She spends most of her time in the Caribbean operating from Miami to various destinations. During the summer she operates in Europe. This image shows her having just arrived in St Maarten. (Darren Holdaway)

The **Emerald Princess** was built in 2007 and has passenger capacity for 3,100. Another Fincantieri yard design for Princess Cruises, she is sister to the **Crown Princess** and **Ruby Princess**. The ship is seen swinging off the berth at Grenada in the Caribbean; she operates from Fort Lauderdale during most of the season while during the British summer months she mainly operates in the Baltic using Copenhagen as her home port. (Darren Holdaway)

Built for P&O Cruises in 2010 at the Fincantieri shipyard in Italy, the **Azura** boasts capacity for over 3,000 passengers. She is seen at her winter turnaround port of Barbados where she operates on a wide range of two-week Caribbean destinations mainly attracting British clientele. (Darren Holdaway)

demographics appealing the most to me with Royal Caribbean and Celebrity. Although my interview was with Royal, it was Celebrity who secured my services with my extensive knowledge in the areas they were looking for. So it was Celebrity I chose and I have no regrets about where I am today.

A few simple paperwork formalities were completed and I was on my way again, this time to Rome and the port of Civitavecchia to prepare for the upcoming Asia season of the *Azamara Quest*. As I boarded this beautiful vessel, I soon felt at home with its stunning surroundings and homely ambiance and I started to prepare all the immigration procedures for this challenging but exciting season in Asia, taking in ports such as Singapore, Hong Kong, Bangkok, Ho Chi Minh City, Beijing, Busan in Korea and Osaka in Japan as well as Taipei.

Many sleepless nights ensued, particularly in one case that I have extremely good (or bad memories of, depending on which way you look at it) on the interesting passage between Hong Kong and Taipei across the South China Sea. The beautiful 'Quest' handles all sea states extremely well. She headed into those seas pitching back and forth to the limit it seemed through the mountainous seas, regardless of her 30,000-ton size and 632 guest count; rolling seems to be non-existent with her.

Captain Carl Smith, born and bred on the Isle of Man, currently Master of the *Azamara Quest*, himself referred to the Ho Chi Minh River as a 'slalom', with its narrow confines, twisting and turning as the ship edged towards the fascinating city ahead. Hong Kong with a beautiful evening sailing, the skies alight with the daily laser show towering above this amazing port, is a perfect setting for any cruise ship sailing out of it and a perfect start to any cruise. The fascinating ports all over Asia are surely a 'must see' for any shipping enthusiast as, in my opinion they are in the most interesting and beautiful part of the world.

After the Asia season was completed, I found myself leaving the ship in Dubai for an extremely long flight to the US to join the *Celebrity Century* and travel with her across to Europe. She was slightly larger than the Azamara brand ships but, yet again, she was another beautiful ship to work and sail on, and it gives me great satisfaction to take a ship from one port to another without any problems. Trans-Atlantic is always a bit special, as it gives me plenty of time to prepare for the arrival into Europe. Generally the first port of entry is either Funchal, Madeira, or Tenerife on the Canary Islands, and I have to make sure all visas are in order for the guests together with the immigration paperwork and that customs papers are up to scratch.

Nowadays, and particularly in the United States, there is an automated system we use called 'APIS' (Advanced Passenger Information System), which is so very important for arrivals into the US. Failure to submit any transmissions can result in the vessel being denied entry and fines, which of course, is always something on my mind.

With the *Celebrity Century* safely in Europe it was time for my vacation and my relief to carry on where I left off. I received my next rotation of ships before I left, so next would be the *Celebrity Infinity*, followed by *Celebrity Solstice*, back to *Celebrity Infinity*, *Celebrity Equinox* and *Celebrity Constellation* where I am now writing this article.

After completing two months leave I found myself joining the latest ship in the Celebrity fleet, the *Celebrity Solstice* which was a far cry from the 30,000-ton *Azamara Quest*. The *Celebrity Solstice* is a fantastic ship in all senses, just like her sisters the *Celebrity Equinox* and *Celebrity Eclipse*. These ships are soon to be joined in the fleet with identical sisters, *Celebrity Silhouette* and *Celebrity Reflection*.

Certain ports in Europe require that all passports be collected at check-

The **Rotterdam** is operated by Holland America Line. She was built by Fincantieri, Italy, in 1997 and has capacity for 1,600 passengers. She is seen stern in at the beautiful Mexican port of Puerta Vallarta during December 2010. (Darren Holdaway)

Built in 2009 at STX Finland, the **Oasis of the Seas** is one of the two largest sisters currently in the Royal Caribbean fleet. She has a gross tonnage of 225,282 and passenger capacity for as many as 5,400 passengers. She is seen here leaving Fort Lauderdale in the US for another seven-day Caribbean cruise during the end of January 2011. (Darren Holdaway)

The **Mein Schiff** was built in Meyer Werft, Papenburg, Germany in 1996 as Celebrity Cruises' **Galaxy**. Passenger capacity is for 1,800 and she operated with Celebrity until 2009 when she was handed over and renamed **Mein Schiff**. This image shows her during a call at Villfranche, France during October 2010. (Darren Holdaway)

*Seen in Barbados are the **Europa** and **Celebrity Constellation**. The Europa was built in 1999 at the Kværner Masa Yards, Finland for Hapag Lloyd. Her capacity is for just 400 passengers. (Darren Holdaway)*

*The train ferry **Mecklenburg Vorpommern** was built in 1996 at the Schichau Seebeckswerft, Bremerhaven yard in Germany for the Rostock-Trelleborg route. She has a passenger capacity for 800 and is seen departing on her 08.00 sailing from Rostock on 16th August 2011.(Darren Holdaway)*

The **Azamara Quest** was built as the **R7** for Renaissance Cruises in 2000 at the Chantiers de l'Atlantique, St. Nazaire yard in France. With a 'guest' capacity for 640 she was renamed in 2003 becoming the **Delphin Renaissance**. After a short spell under this name, in 2006 she was renamed **Blue Moon**. In 2007 she was handed over to Royal Caribbean to form the Azamara Cruises brand and was named **Azamara Quest**. During 2010 Azamara Cruises rebranded their product and now the company operates separately as Azamara Club Cruises. The 'Quest' spends most of her cruising itineraries in the Mediterranean and Asia. In this image she is seen leaving Piraeus, Greece on 17th September 2011. (Darren Holdaway)

The **Star Princess** and **Baltic Princess** are seen during July 2011 at Helsinki. The 'Star' is seen at her berth loading for Tallinn, whilst the **Baltic Princess** has just arrived. The 'Star' was built in 2007 by the Aker yards in Helsinki and has an impressive service speed of 27 knots. The **Baltic Princess** was built at the Aker yards in St Nazaire, France in 2008 and has a passenger capacity for 2,800 passengers and service speed of 24 knots. (Darren Holdaway)

in which is always one of my dislikes but has to be done. You have to plan ahead and see where the ship is heading to or from, particularly if you are going in and out of Schengen countries, Turkey to Greece for example, or when in Asia from Japan to China and back to Japan or vice versa.

For me, a typical day at present would start at 06.00 or sometimes earlier depending on the arrival time into port. I like to be up and around in time for the pilot station, at which time the pilot boards and takes the ship into port. A pilot could come on and ask for a particular document, so I always like to be around if this is the case. Final preparation is then made for arrival; customs paperwork and the stores declaration are printed and pieced together ready for arrival, as well as other documents, which I generally prepare the night before. Each port is different and has its own requirements, so it's up to me to find this out ahead of time to prepare for the upcoming itinerary. A new itinerary is always a challenge, as you never know what to expect when arriving into a new port. I report directly on board to the Guest Relations Manager, who is in charge of the day-to-day operation of the Guest Relations Desk and guest issues. He or she would in this case make sure everything is in place and ready, although nowadays I am left to my own work, which gives me great satisfaction to know that they have the knowledge and confidence in me to be aware that everything will be in order.

Once in port I meet with the local authorities, immigration, customs, health officials and the local port agent on the gangway and take them to the clearance room on the ship, where the clearance of arrival is performed. Generally after a few minutes and once everything is in order, clearance is given and guests and crew can go ashore. I can either find myself running around like a chicken or otherwise doing nothing. Generally most ports have the same procedure but this can vary, particularly in the challenging ports of Asia, where requirements are met, and they then decide to change their minds when we arrive and want something completely different.

After an early start, my shift would then finish at around 11.00, depending on whether there is anything pending. After a short break it is usually back again for two to three hours prior to departure to prepare the departure formalities and preparation for the next arrival. My day would generally finish at around 19.00 (if sailing is at 18.00 for example). The cruise ships are a little more relaxed on the alcohol policy, unlike ferries where the alcohol policy is zero tolerance which obviously came into effect after the Zeebrugge disaster. Each and every one of them has their own company policies to adhere to which are handed out to crew members when joining a vessel. Each crew member is then sent through an induction course which is held on board going through various emergency signals, plans, muster stations and instructions for watertight doors and the operation of fire extinguishing appliances and such like.

Travelling around these ports on beautiful ships also gives me the opportunity to photograph other ships around the world and in port. Whether it be ferries, cruise ships, cargo ships, tenders or car carriers, it gives me so much pleasure to be part of this fascinating world of shipping, and to be involved with the cruise ship industry.

*The **Aida Blu** was built in 2010 at the Jos. L. Meyer, Papenburg yard in Germany for Aida Cruises. She has a passenger capacity for 2,050, and is seen at the cruise terminal at Wernamunde, Germany during one of her turnaround calls in the summer of 2011. (Darren Holdaway)*

*The **Birka Paradise** is seen passing through the archipelago, approaching Stockholm during a bright afternoon on 7th June 2011. She was built in 2004 by Aker Finnyards Oy, Rauma, Finland and operates for Birka Cruises with a capacity for 1,800 passengers. (Darren Holdaway)*

*Built in 2001 as the **Superfast V** for Superfast Ferries at the Howaldtswerke Deutsche Werft AG, Kiel yard, Germany, the ship operated between Patras and Ancona in 2001 and various other routes in the Mediterranean including Patras-Igoumenitsa-Bari service. She later was acquired by Brittany Ferries and as the **Cap Finistere**. She is seen arriving in Portsmouth harbour on 27th March from refit in Poland to take up the new Bilbao service. (Darren Holdaway)*

6

The Saga Family
by Nigel Thornton

In 1948, Sidney de Hann achieved his ambition to run a small seaside hotel when he purchased the Rhodesia Hotel in Folkestone, Kent. Realising that holidaymakers did not come to the town outside the summer season and noticing the large number of retired people who visited the south-east during the off-peak, he decided to offer 'all inclusive' holidays especially aimed at this market. So began Saga which he founded in 1951.

Prior to this, de Haan had already identified three critical factors under which he wished his company to operate. Firstly, to concentrate exclusively on older customers. Secondly, to market to them 'direct' and thirdly to offer them value for money. In essence, he aimed to offer guests that family feel rather than treating them as just mere customers.

Saga's first venture abroad was in 1959 when they launched 'No passport day trips' to France. However, together with all their other investments, it wasn't until 1996 that Saga purchased their first cruise ship, the *Saga Rose* (ex *Sagafjord*). Built in 1965 (24,002 gross tons) the 'Rose' always had a bit of 'style' about her and heads turned wherever she went. Whenever I saw her, she always appeared stately and moved with the grace of an ageing figure skater; speedy in a straight line and slow in the turns. Occasionally she needed help.

The ship came from a good background and was always well turned out. Most of her fittings were dark and of good quality. Towards the end of her 45-year career though, she began to show her age, but what would you have expected from a ship that still managed to sail around the world each year?

In 2003 Saga added to the fleet and purchased the 'Ruby' (ex *Vistafjord*). Being eight years her sister's junior she looked sharper than the 'Rose' but although related, did not have the same origin. She has fine flowing lines and also boasts a well-rounded superstructure. She too continues to embark on an annual world cruise.

The year 2003 also saw the company add the *Saga Pearl* to their fleet. This ship was originally intended to be the Soviet research vessel *Okean* (built by Okean Shipyard, Nikolaiew – yard number 1) but her 1989-built hull was purchased by V-Ships who towed her from Ukraine to Italy, where she was converted into a ship tailored to the requirements of Swan Hellenic Cruises. She was officially named *Minerva* in June 1996 and began cruising for Swan Hellenic. Her charter to Saga as the *Saga Pearl* commenced in May 2003. This lasted for six months of each year up until 2005 and although totally different in appearance, with a squarely balanced profile and a shallower draft, she was a valued family member offering alternative, unusual destinations.

The *Spirit of Adventure* (ex *Berlin*) was acquired in 2006. Built in 1980 by Howaldtswerke-Deutsche Werft, Kiel, (Yard No. 163 of 7,813 gross tons), she was of similar draft to the *Saga Pearl*. She sails under her own branding but still with the friendly emphasis which Sidney de Haan did so much to encourage all those years ago.

In December 2009 the *Saga Rose* left Southampton for the final time and sadly headed for the scrapyard. However, in 2010 along came the *Saga Pearl II* (ex *Astoria*). She was built in 1981 at Howaldtswerke-Deutsche Werft,

The view from the **Saga Ruby**'s bridge looking forward across her lengthy fo'c'sle which not only provides the ship with classic lines but also comfortable voyages for Saga's customers. (John Hendy)

Germany (yard number 165) initially of 18,591 gross tons and with an intended name of *Hammonia*. Her owners, Transocean Tours went into liquidation and she was purchased, at auction, by Saga Shipping. Arriving in Swansea in September 2009 she underwent a £20 million refit and refurbishment.

Being totally different in exterior appearance to anything previously seen within the Saga family, with her sharp lines, angular funnel and with a different type of pedigree, she too has become well respected and extremely popular amongst her followers.

What of the future? In May 2012, the *Saga Pearl II* is expected to replace the *Spirit of Adventure* and become *Quest for Adventure* and, of course, the *Saga Sapphire* (ex *Bleu de France*) will enter service in March 2012. She was originally built in 1981 at Bremer Vulkan, Vegesack, Bremen (yard number 1001). Initially of 33,819 gross tons, she will undergo a multimillion contemporary refurbishment. The company claims that "She is going to be radically different from anything that's come before!"

Will the Saga family change? I expect so, but, in my opinion, only for the better. Finally, speaking of the ships past, present and future, one of the regular Masters once said, "I know it's a cliché, when you say it's a family, but that's what it is. You have to experience it!"

*The **Saga Ruby**'s forward stairwell provides a futuristic view down through the ship. (John Hendy)*

*In her original Norwegian America Line livery, the **Saga Rose** as the **Sagafjord**. Built by FCM at La Seyne-sur-Mer in 1964, the ship completed her maiden trans-Atlantic crossing in October 1965. Sold to Cunard in May 1983, the vessel eventually passed to Saga in 1997, operating her inaugural cruise from Dover in May of that year. (FotoFlite)*

*The **Vistafjord** (**Saga Ruby**) at speed in the English Channel. The ship was a product of the Swan Hunter yard at Wallsend-on-Tyne, operating her maiden voyage from Oslo to New York in May 1973. With her near sister, she passed to Cunard in 1983 later being renamed **Caronia**. Saga acquired her in 2004 and she operated her first cruise for her new owners from Southampton in March 2005. (FotoFlite)*

The **Saga Rose** was finally withdrawn from service in 2009 and although there were hopes that she would be saved from the breakers, she was eventually dismantled in China. The addition of cabins on top of her bridge did little to hide her classic lines. (Nigel Thornton)

The **Saga Ruby** represents the final chapter in the construction of British passenger ships and although she was primarily built for cruising, her lines are unmistakably those of an Atlantic liner. (Nigel Thornton)

*A burst from the 9-cylinder 9RD68 Sulzer diesels of the **Saga Ruby** signals her departure from Dover. This view gives a fine impression of the ship's tiered after decks which provide views astern, shelter and comfort for her cruise customers. She is now registered in Valletta (Malta). (Nigel Thornton)*

*Dressed overall and looking every inch a 'classic' the **Saga Rose**. (Nigel Thornton)*

*Looking astern from the **Saga Ruby**'s port bridge wing during a lay-over in Dover. (John Hendy)*

*The **Saga Ruby**'s bridge is a mixture of old and new. The wooden-clad, brass-topped binnacle is a reminder of her early days. (John Hendy)*

The **Saga Ruby** at Southampton on 1st November 2011 with P&O Cruises' **Aurora** in the background, pending her deperature to Madeira. (Miles Cowsill)

*The comfortable South Cape Bar in the **Saga Ruby** is situated on her forward port side. (John Hendy)*

*Conventional panelling and leather 'wing-back' reading chairs were the hallmarks of the well-stocked **Saga Rose** library. (Nigel Thornton)*

*In the summer of 2003, the **Saga Pearl** (ex **Okean** and currently the **Minerva**) begins her swing off the berth at Dover's Cruise Terminal 1. The ship was chartered by Saga for the summer seasons between 2003-05 and was a radically different vessel to the 'Rose' and the 'Ruby'. (Nigel Thornton)*

*Prior to departure, the **Saga Pearl** off the berth at Cruise Terminal 1. With a hull built in 1989, it was not until 1996 that the former Soviet research ship finally entered service for Swan Hellenic. (Nigel Thornton)*

The library of the **Saga Pearl II** showing her new, contemporary styling which is already a favourite with her passengers. (Nigel Thornton)

The Dining Room of the **Saga Rose** showing her luxurious blue colour scheme with elegant traditional fittings. (Nigel Thornton)

The clean cut design and open seating of the **Saga Pearl II** *Dining Room. (Nigel Thornton)*

The **Saga Pearl II** *(ex* **Astoria***) basking in the afternoon sunshine. Built in Germany as the* **Astoria** *during 1981, the ship was acquired by Saga in 2009 and following a £20 million refit in Swansea, joined the fleet in the following year. In 2012 she will become the* **Quest for Adventure***, replacing the 'Spirit' under the Spirit of Adventure branding. (John Mavin)*

Being of 9,570 gross tons and comparing her with the Dover Harbour Board tug **DHB Doughty**, *it is quite apparent that being smaller than most cruise liners, the* **Spirit of Adventure** *is able to visit destinations which many of her competitors cannot. With a need for greater capacity in 2012, the* **Quest for Adventure** *(ex* **Saga Pearl II**) *will be her instant, effective replacement when she sails on for FTI Cruises as* **FTI Berlin**. *(Nigel Thornton)*

After entering the Fincantieri yard at Palermo in November 2011, Croisières de France's **Bleu de France** *will undergo a 15 million Euros refit and will emerge in February 2012 as the* **Saga Sapphire**. *Her inaugural cruise will commence in Southampton on 26th March 2012 at which time she will become the company's fourth ship. (Saga)*

The **Saga Pearl II** *cruising in the English Channel showing her immaculate paintwork and ample outside deck space to full advantage. (FotoFlite)*

7

The Gosport Ferries
by Andrew Cooke

Visitors to Portsmouth Harbour cannot fail to overlook the presence of the green-hulled passenger ferries that ply the historic route between Gosport's waterfront and Portsea, Portsmouth. Operated by the Gosport Ferry Ltd, the ferries continue a long and proud tradition linking the town of Gosport and the city of Portsmouth across Portsmouth Harbour in the shadow of the history-rich Naval Dockyard. In its heyday the service conveyed around 10 million passengers per annum but, as road links to Gosport improved and car and bus usage increased, the annual footfall figures declined by around two thirds. The cross-harbour link has continued through relentless change to its surroundings and now exists in the shadow of high-rise housing and the iconic Spinnaker Tower.

ANCESTRY

The ferry service can trace its ancestry back to when the watermen's trade was originally regulated by order of the Court of the Exchequer in 1603 and by 1664 the operation was provided by the wherrymen. At this time the boat operators were known by this name as their small rowing boats were known as wherries. Two primary routes existed from Gosport to Point (Old Portsmouth) and Portsmouth Hard (Portsea) near the entrance to the sprawling Naval Dockyard. The industry was very much run by families and therefore a closed operation to outsiders.

Overcharging became rife and this forced an Act of Parliament in 1809 to regulate the fare structure. Such a structure was not maintained until 1835 with the watermen's 200-year monopoly being challenged in 1840 with the arrival of the chain ferry. The proposal was tabled in 1838 and was met with fierce opposition from the watermen. Nevertheless the chain ferry service, operated by the steam-powered *Victoria*, commenced in May 1840 operating every 15 minutes for 14 hours a day. The arrival of the railway in Gosport boosted the popularity of the service with a second vessel, the *Albert*, quickly joining the initial craft. Both were eventually replaced by the *Alexandra* and *Duchess of York* powered by internal combustion engines. By the 1950s, their usage declined, repair costs soared and the end came in 1959. Ironically such a service would be of great use in the 21st century due to congestion on the A32 into Gosport. Sadly of course this would be prohibited by the logistics, costs and limited land availability whilst the much discussed tramway tunnel was scrapped soon after the dawn of the new Millennium.

The era of the floating bridge prompted the rival boatmen to invest in

*The vehicle and passenger chain ferry **Duchess of York** is depicted at Portsmouth Point awaiting a passage to Gosport. The passenger ferries can be seen going about their business; the chain ferry ceased in 1959. (www.simplonpc.co.uk)*

steam-powered launches with such craft then also supplementing the existing service offered by The Floating Bridge Company. By 1870 much of the trade had been re-captured by the watermen but the competition was hard fought. In 1875 a group of watermen joined forces to form the Gosport & Portsea Watermen's Steam Launch Company (GPWSL Co.) utilising four steam launches. Most of this company's steam craft were built by Gosport-based Camper & Nicholson.

COMPETITION

The railway was extended to Portsmouth Harbour station in 1876 thus handing the boatmen a wealth of new clients via the accompanying free public landing stage. The success of the GPWSL Co. prompted the formation of the rival Port of Portsmouth Steam Launch and Towing Company (PPSLT Co.) in 1883. Shares in this operation, which soon became known as the 'New Company', were bought by local watermen and businessmen. They promptly placed three steam launches, all built by Edwards & Symes of Millwall, on the same route as their rivals which were duly dubbed the 'Old Company'.

The design of launch utilised by both operators was largely similar. They offered a safety chain lined foredeck, which was level with the landing stages, where bicycles and standing passengers were accommodated plus an open steering position forward of the funnel. The main deck was raised and provided seating whilst below decks was cramped accommodation for use during inclement weather. These workhorses found further employment when replaced with the design altering little in 80 years, except for a change to diesel propulsion in the 1950s.

Back in 1884 the 'New Company' agreed to build two further launches whilst competition between both operators reached fever pitch. Four years later a co-ordinated service was agreed between the rivals with vessels from both companies sailing alternately to share the passengers. The Floating Bridge Company launches had continued to serve the Point with their trade declining as the emphasis on the new city centre grew. A limited number of independent watermen continue to ply Portsmouth Harbour to this day (tourist sightseeing etc.) but both rival companies soaked up the majority at an early stage.

Immediately prior to the Second World War came a major step forward when the likes of the *Ferry Prince* of 1937 and the *Vadne* of 1939 took to the water for the 'Old' and 'New' companies respectively. The latter was actually the first ferry to be built by Vosper's Portsmouth yard and was quickly gathered up by the Examination Service for war duties. She was shipped out to Freetown in West Africa for tendering duties, a far cry from her intended career as a humble cross-harbour ferry. However, once the hostilities around the globe had subsided, the little *Vadne* was sent back home.

The one vessel not to return after the war was the 1900-built *Sandringham*. She was employed by the Port of Portsmouth Floating Bridge Company, mainly on excursion work, and replaced the *Eva Mary* in service. She was used by the War Department and was not released until 1956 when she was sold to Solent Blue Line (later Blue Funnel Cruises) for local excursions. She was fitted with Gardner engines and ran until 1969 when her engines were donated to the last operational steam ferry, *Venus*.

The post-war era kicked off with two new vessels in 1948. The *Ferry Princess* and *Venus* were delivered to the Old Company and New Company respectively. Both were spawned from Gosport's Camper & Nicholson yard and maintained the tradition of 'Ferry' prefix names for the Old Company and 'V' names for the New Company.

The vehicle and passenger chain ferry **Alexandra** is shown crossing Portsmouth Harbour from Gosport to Old Portsmouth in 1953. Unlike their predecessors, these second generation ferries were fitted with internal combustion engines. (John H. Meredith)

The location is unconfirmed but the vessel is the **Viceroy** that was built in 1902 and operated until 1929. Spare craft frequently undertook summer excursions across the Solent to destinations such as Ryde and Seaview. This veteran craft finally ended her career as a houseboat. (Gosport Ferry Ltd)

The **Verda** was built in 1929 for service across Portsmouth Harbour but is shown here on an excursion as the location is in the area of the Swashway channel with Fort Blockhouse as a backdrop. These wonderfully versatile yet basic craft were a joy to behold. The **Verda** also became a houseboat. (www.simplonpc.co.uk)

*The style and spirit of the post-war Gosport Ferries is demonstrated by this view of the 1959-built **Ferry Queen** captured on sea trials in the Solent. She was built by Camper & Nicholson in Gosport and was diesel powered. After 15 years' service she moved to the Thames and was sold as a houseboat in 2009. (Beken of Cowes)*

*The **Varos** was built in 1929 and served her owners until replaced in 1952. She then found employment with the now Blue Funnel Cruises Ltd at Southampton. Shown here at Southampton's Royal Pier, the vessel had received a glazed cabin, imitation funnel and covered seating aft for her new role. After 22 years the former ferry found new employment on the Thames. (www.simplonpc.co.uk)*

*The **Venus** took to the water in 1948 and was photographed at the Gosport ferry pontoon in 1966 after withdrawal. The last steamer was eventually sold to Thames Pleasure Craft in 1968. At the ferry berth can be seen one of the brand new 'Queens' whilst the backdrop is dominated by the Gunwharf Power Station and HMS **Vernon**. This area is now home to the Wightlink car ferry terminal and Gunwharf Quays. (John Hendy)*

The *Vesta II* (so called as another non-ferry vessel carried this name locally) was retired at this time. She moved to the Thames in 1948 for Mrs C. Hastings of Kingston. She was re-engined as a diesel and renamed *Kingston Belle* in 1949, ownership passing to H.G. Hastings, who owned her until 1954. In 1963 she returned to the Solent for Southampton Pleasure Cruises but was out of service by 1982.

Times were changing and in 1954 the 'Old Company' sought professional advice as to which direction to take when choosing the propulsive power for the next series of ferries. The advice was to remain with steam but instead use triple expansion engines and oil-fired boilers. So, in 1959 the splendid *Ferry Queen* was born, courtesy of Camper & Nicholson at a cost of £43,832 and fitted with a diesel engine! Perhaps this was no surprise as the 'New Company' had produced the diesel-powered *Vesta* in 1956. This duo was followed up by the *Vita* in 1960. The *Ferry Queen (1)*, *Ferry King*, *Varos* and *Verda* were all retired between 1950 and 1960 and each found further work on the Solent or Thames.

ONE COMPANY – TWO QUEENS

The 1950s saw the instigation by the 'New Company' of a proposed amalgamation with their rivals. The process seemed to lack enthusiasm as it was not completed until 1962 despite the obvious benefits to both concerns. In 1957 the Floating Bridge Company had mounted one last bid for survival by proposing a proper car ferry service across the harbour but this received a lukewarm reception and two years later the operation carried its last passenger. In 1961 the 'New Company' evolved into the Portsmouth Harbour Ferry Company (PHFC), the 'Old Company' was swallowed up and the single company went into the following year with a whole new outlook. Cost-saving measures included the loss of ten staff members, the off peak service reduced to three boats from four, deck controls were fitted with a view to dispensing with engineers and the overall fleet size was cut from eight to seven by disposing of the 1924-built *Ferry Belle* as she was in the poorest condition. A new series of excursions to the Isle of Wight also commenced in conjunction with Southern Vectis and Red Funnel. The pace of progress was gathering speed and next to come under the spotlight was the future fleet requirement of the PHFC. The need for larger and more economical vessels to cut costs and boost the profit margins became clear with a revolutionary design by Mr W.J. Ayers of James Dewar & Sons winning the day.

The new design was a far cry from the smaller ferries with an almost full-length covered deck, outer deck above with seating plus a fully enclosed wheelhouse above this level. The enclosed deck comprised of seating on the starboard side/forward and a large area for standing passengers plus bicycles/motorbikes and their riders. The stern area also offered open-air seating. Each vessel was to cost £75,000 with around £100,000 required by the PHFC by way of a loan. The economic climate dictated that a loan was not forthcoming from the banks but one of the favoured shipyards stepped forward with a solution. Messrs J.I. Thornycroft of Woolston offered a funding package that the PHFC welcomed with open arms. The two new 30.5 metre long vessels were quickly underway as Yard Nos. 4211/4212 made history by being launched simultaneously into the River Itchen during April 1966. Christened the *Portsmouth Queen* and *Gosport Queen*, the 169 gross ton ferries offered a capacity of 500 passengers with dedicated embarkation (forward) and disembarkation (aft) points to accelerate turnaround times. An engine located at either end of each vessel provides power for the two Schottel rudder-propeller units that can be turned 360 degrees thus providing excellent manoeuvrability.

Here we see the New Company's **Vadne** *on launch day in 1939 at Vosper's Portsmouth Yard. This proud little vessel almost immediately found herself being shipped to West Africa for use as a Naval tender during WWII. She survived to return home for the purpose she was built for and served until 1965. Alas her intended use with Gosport Cruising Club failed to materialise and she remains derelict at Forton Lake, Gosport, the only example of her generation to survive locally. (Gosport Ferry Ltd)*

The **Ferry Belle** *was built in 1924 and is shown here alongside the Portsea pontoon awaiting passengers. In the background is the unmistakable landmark of the Semaphore Tower, built 1913, and the masts of HMS* **Victory.** *The railway bridge to the Naval Dockyard is, like the ferry herself, now a distant memory. The* **Ferry Belle** *moved to the Thames upon withdrawal in 1966. (John H. Meredith)*

An unidentified Gosport Ferry heads away from the Portsea pontoon on another cross-harbour trip in the early post-war era and passes the second of the British Railway Portsmouth-Ryde passenger ferries, **Brading**, *at the Portsmouth Harbour Station berth. The* **Brading** *was built in 1948 and was withdrawn in 1986. (www.simplonpc.co.uk)*

Three chapters of the Gosport Ferry service are shown here at the Gosport pontoon. The 2001-built **Spirit of Gosport** *departs as the 1966-built* **Gosport Queen** *approaches. At the inner berth is the 1971-built* **Solent Enterprise**. *Built as a ferry and excursion/party vessel she was delivered as the* **Gay Enterprise** *and was sold for service on the Thames in 2005. Having moved to Denmark in 2008 the craft is now a B&B and cafe venue. (Andrew Cooke)*

Both ferries made their debut on 29th October 1966 although the usual teething problems did generate early criticism. One unfortunate occasion saw the *Portsmouth Queen* fail during the rush hour with the little ferries and the *Gosport Queen* left struggling to then clear an estimated queue of 1,200 passengers. The *Vesta* (1956) and *Vita* (1960) were entrusted with the relief duties during the annual refits of the 'Queens' until a third new generation vessel arrived. In 1971 the *Gay Enterprise* was delivered and was a larger version of her new fleet companions offering a dual role of ferry and party/sightseeing cruiser. Equipped with an upper saloon, bar, galley and dance floor, the vessel offered Solent cruises during the summer before being stripped of her cruise fittings each winter for use as a Gosport ferry. The vessel was renamed *Solent Enterprise* after a few years and served her owners faithfully until 2005.

Meanwhile, back in 1974 the PHFC trio were joined by the slightly more attractive but smaller excursion vessel *Southsea Queen*. The fourth of the PHFC quartet enjoyed a brief chapter in the company's history before she was sold in 1978 to become the Southampton-Hythe ferry *Hythe Hotspur*.

Successors to the original watermen continued to offer trips around Portsmouth Harbour from the Portsea pontoon and from the beach near Clarence Pier in Southsea. In the mid-1980s they formed Portsmouth Harbour Tours, and subsequently began operating a circular waterbus service around the attractions of Portsmouth Harbour. The boats remained owned by the individuals, but proceeds were shared between them proportionate to the number of boats deployed. All boats received a pale blue livery and are often referred to as the 'Blue Boats'. The PHFC initially joined this consortium, using two 'Blue Boats' of their own, the *Solent Prince* and *Solent Princess* but due to limited returns, the company pulled out of this arrangement in 1996. A 60 passenger capacity launch, the *Solent Prince (II)* joined the fleet in the 1990s and has since found her way to Solent & Wightline Cruises.

Back on the frontline, the two 'Queens' quickly gained an excellent reputation in service and have led fairly uneventful lives since. Hiccups have occurred such as the freak incident in 1980 when both vessels became simultaneously entangled in the same rope trailing from a passing barge as they crossed the harbour in either direction. The disabled ferries were quickly rescued by other craft. The passenger fleet would remain unchanged until the dawn of the new Millennium but the pontoons that the ferries serve were less robust. As British Rail could not afford to maintain it, the pontoon at Portsea eventually passed to the control of the PHFC via the Portsea Harbour Company Act in 1984. The pontoon was renewed to its present form at the end of 1989. The layout of Gosport's waterfront began to take shape as early as 1922 and from 1919 the ferry companies paid fixed charges to use the pontoon facility. Ownership of this was retained by Gosport Borough Council and in 1982 Hampshire County Council successfully sought to amend the act so that the PHFC paid maintenance charges governed by the volume of ferry traffic. Renewal work at Gosport's pontoon was completed in 1982 but a storm in 1989 severely damaged the structure and made it inoperable for several weeks. Until repairs were completed, operations diverted to Clarence Yard in Gosport and this proved highly unpopular.

NEW SPIRIT – NEW ERA

Until 1988, the PHFC was in a comfortable position but a tempestuous period was to follow that would leave the company's future in serious doubt. The acquisition of a second Travel Agency and a marine business at

A landmark event in the history of the Gosport Ferry service was the launching of sister vessels **Portsmouth Queen** *and* **Gosport Queen** *at Vosper Thornycroft's Woolston yard in Southampton during April 1966. These ferries have now achieved over 45 years of frontline service, a remarkable achievement. The waterfront of Portsmouth Harbour has changed significantly in this period, but these faithful little ships remain. (Gosport Ferry Ltd)*

Having settled down into their duties, the **Portsmouth Queen** *and* **Gosport Queen** *are shown here at Gosport in the 1970s resplendent in their initial PHF livery. The* **Portsmouth Queen** *is in service whilst her sister is laying over prior to resuming the peak hours service. (Ian Boyle)*

The manoeuvrability of the 1966-built 'Queens' is demonstrated in this view of the **Portsmouth Queen** *departing from the Portsea pontoon during May 1992. The livery is the modified "double arrow" emblem version that remains to this day. Behind the vessel is P&O European Ferries'* **Pride of Winchester** *departing for Cherbourg. The 'Queens' have witnessed remarkable changes in Portsmouth's cross-Channel scene. (Andrew Cooke)*

Port Solent generated intolerable drains on the company's finances and this was closely followed by losses incurred by the damaged Gosport pontoon in 1989. The Board of Directors then faced a takeover bid for PHFC by Whitehorse Ferries in 1994 (operators of the Hythe-Southampton ferry) but, following a major shake-up of both the board and internal matters, a new business plan was presented to and accepted by the shareholders thus defeating any takeover. By 1997 the company was beginning to emerge from the stabilisation process and was performing well. However, a new proposal for a tramway tunnel under Portsmouth Harbour had surfaced but the PHFC's plans for a new generation of ferries could be postponed no longer. To guarantee ongoing reliability a new ferry design was sought with the design contract going to Camarc Ltd of Worthing. The construction contract for what would become the *Spirit of Gosport* was awarded to Abel's Shipbuilders Ltd of Bristol in May 2000 with the 300 gross ton and 32.6 metre long vessel being delivered in April 2001. The process did not go as smoothly as anticipated with the new ferry arriving at Gosport with, reportedly, in excess of 100 faults. Two Scania D9M turbo charged engines each drive a Veth 360 degree azimuthing propulsion unit located fore and aft providing a service speed of 12 knots. The layout of the 300 passenger capacity vessel is broadly similar to the 1966-built 'Queens' but the 'Spirit' is also equipped with a full width bridge. The two raked funnels, located on the top deck, are not exhaust uptakes as these are located in the stern.

In the same year, the Portsmouth Harbour Ferry Company Limited (PHFC) became the Portsmouth Harbour Ferry Company PLC, a holding company for various subsidiaries, one of which is Gosport Ferry Limited, which continues to run the ferries. This change came about following a fairly lively takeover by Falkland Island Holdings and the pale green livery was darkened slightly to reflect the change of ownership. The *Spirit of Gosport* operated harbour cruises during the 2001 International Festival of

*The 1939-built **Vadne,** having been abandoned at Forton Lake, Gosport, after her post ferry career plans failed. The only example of this series of ferry to remain in home waters, this little ship has long since lost the ability to float but remains defiant to the elements. (Andrew Cooke)*

the Sea and was formally named in Gosport on 4th October 2001 by Mrs Gillian Wright, wife of the Chairman. The 'Queens' continued their frontline service in a four-strong fleet whilst the original order for a *Spirit of Portsmouth* at Abel's Shipbuilders was abandoned due to various issues. The partly built vessel remains there in 2011.

In June 2005 a successful attempt to build the second 'Spirit' saw the vessel enter service just in time for the huge Trafalgar 200 and International Festival of the Sea event. The 377 gross ton vessel's hull was prefabricated in Holland and fitting out was completed at Vosper Thornycroft's Porchester yard with who the contract was placed. The second vessel mirrors her sister except for an upper deck saloon, bar and galley. Her

*The two 'Queens' have served through all manner of occasions in Portsmouth Harbour and this June 2004 view shows the **Portsmouth Queen** at work on the 60th Anniversary of the D-Day landings. The crowds lining the waterfront at Gosport were awaiting the departure of a Naval flotilla bound for Normandy. (Andrew Cooke)*

LIFE AFTER THE GOSPORT FERRY – THE STEAM & DIESEL GENERATIONS

Name	Period of Service	Sold To
Sandringham	1900-1941	1956 Solent Blue Line. Ran until 1969.
Duke of York	1900-1929	Built for the Gosport & Portsea Watermen's Steam Launch Co. by Camper & Nicholson. Also served Buckler's Hard – fate unknown.
Viceroy	1902-1929	1929-1946 George Wheeler Launches, River Thames., 1946-1964 PJ & RF Jackson of Hammersmith. 1965-1970 Thames Launches. 1971-1980 Jackson Bros – 1981 River Rides Ltd. Ended her career as a houseboat on the River Medway. *
Vesta II	1909-1948	1948 Mrs C. Hastings of Kingston. Renamed *Kingston Belle* in 1949. Operated by H.G. Hastings until 1954. Southampton Pleasure Cruises 1963-1982.
Ferry Queen (1)	1908-1956	Doug House of Ryde in 1956, renamed *Wight Queen*. Passed to a Nejieris Yiallouros on the Thames in the 1970s. She remains as a houseboat at Brentford. *
Ferry King	1918-1962	Solent Queen 1962 to 1984 – Solent Boating Company (later Blue Funnel Cruises) – *Crystal Rose* 1985 to 2005 – Hayden & Scott, Waterford. Ferry King 2005 to date – M. Byrne, Wexford – under restoration. *
Princessa	1921-1958	1958 - Solent Boating Co. Employed on Southampton Water & Beaulieu River until 1986 when sold to operate in Falmouth. Passed to Falmouth Pleasure Cruises in 2001. *
Ferry Belle	1924-1966	Sold 1965 to John Coakley on the Thames, running between Westminster, Tower Pier and Greenwich. In 1981 she was running for Pearltarn along with the *Varos*.
Varos	1929-1952	Solent Boating Co. (Blue Funnel Cruises) & withdrawn 1974 Coakley's Launches 1976, Ran Westminster/Tower Pier to Greenwich.
Verda	1929-1958	Sold 1950 to Solent Boating Co. Survived in 2008 as houseboat at Shoreham. *
Ferry Prince	1937-1966	To Thames Pleasure Craft in 1966. She was dieselised in 1967.
Vadne	1939-1965	Gosport Cruising Club. Derelict at Forton Lake, Gosport. *
Venus	1948-1966	1968 – Solent Boating Co. 1978 – Greenwich Pleasure Craft. Now based in Brisbane, Australia as a commercial passenger vessel but has rigging and sails for use as a two-masted sailing vessel. *
Ferry Princess	1948-1968	Sold 1968 to Thames Pleasure Craft.
Vesta	1956-1974	Sold to Thames Pleasure Craft in 1974. 1977 – Thames Launches. 1978 – Arthur Green as *Duchess M* and then D.C & W. Tours in 1981. By 1983 *Duchess M* was under the Capital Cruises banner. In 1991 she was on the River Tyne running charter cruises for Rolls Royce Limousine Hire, passing to River Tyne Cruises by 1995. In 1997 *Duchess M* was back on the Thames at Southend. Sold 2002 to the Lower Thames & Medway Passenger Boat Co. for use on the Tilbury-Gravesend ferry, where she remains. *
Ferry Queen	1959-1974	Sold to Thames Pleasure Craft, where she ran with the other ex-Gosport ferries *Ferry Prince* and *Ferry Princess*. To City Cruises c.1995 until 2006. Sales listed and still employed in 2007. Sold 2009 as a houseboat. *
Vita	1960-1974	To Woods Cruises for use on the Thames, passing to City Cruises c.1999. Sold 2009 as a houseboat. *
Solent Enterprise	1971-2005	Built as the Gay Enterprise. Sold 2005 to Capital Pleasure. Boats on the Thames – renamed *Sundance*. Sold to Danish interests as a houseboat in autumn 2008. *
Southsea Queen	1974-1978	Sold 1978 to the Hythe-Southampton ferry service as the *Hythe Hotspur*. Withdrawn 1995 and chartered to Brownsea Island Ferries, adopting their yellow livery. Sold to Blue Funnel in 1996 as their *Poole Scene*. Sold to Clyde Marine Services as the *Cruiser* in 1999 where she remains. 119t/200 passengers. *

*- The former British passenger vessel SUNDANCE is now a static café and bed and breakfast in Svendborg, Denmark. **Note:** Six ex-Gosport ferries were serving on the River Thames to/from Greenwich in 1977.

*The **Spirit of Gosport** was delivered by Abel's of Bristol in 2001 and represented a 21st century version of the 1966-built sisters. She remains unique and can generally still be seen in service with one of the 'Queens'. A larger multi-purpose version of the first 'Spirit' arrived in the form of the **Spirit of Portsmouth** in 2005. (Andrew Cooke)*

cruise mode lacks much in the way of frills and so the *Spirit of Portsmouth* can easily switch between her ferry and leisure roles. The vessel was named at Clarence Yard on 11th May 2005.

The previous cruise vessel *Solent Enterprise* was sold out of the fleet in April 2005 and moved to the River Thames for Capital Pleasure Boats (CPB) where she was renamed *Sundance*. This role was short-lived and she was sold to Danish interests in 2007, leaving the Thames under her own power on 10th October that year for conversion to a stylish houseboat. Interestingly her time at CPB saw her join former Southampton-based vessels *Leisure Scene* (Blue Funnel Cruises) and *New Forester* (Hythe Ferries) now known as the *Golden Jubilee* and *Golden Star*.

July 2009 saw the departure from the Thames of the final two former Gosport ferries in service on the river when the *Vita* and *Ferry Queen* sailed to Grimsby for conversion into houseboats.

RETROSPECT

The 6-cylinder Gardener engines of the faithful *Portsmouth Queen* and *Gosport Queen* (now with a capacity for 250 passengers) have now echoed across the waters of Portsmouth Harbour providing frontline service for 45 years and a time when neither vessel plays a part in the harbour scene seems unthinkable. Minor modifications have been undertaken here and there during their careers including new staircases located aft between the promenade deck and main deck. The original stairways were narrow and steep with only the aft one in a location where modification was possible. Strictly speaking the outside deck also has a 'one way' flow of passengers towards the stern and passengers are not permitted to undertake 'non landing' trips.

The 'Queens' and 'Spirits' continue to work in harmony to maintain the service from 05.30 to midnight, 364 days a year. The two-boat peak service provides sailings every seven and a half minutes and the off peak single

vessel service running every 15 minutes. Around 3.8 million passengers use the service annually with some of the former fleet members still employed on active duties. A handful of vessels have succumbed as houseboats (hideous or otherwise) and let us not forget the diminutive *Vadne* that sits rotting away at Forton Lake, Gosport and serves as a final reminder of the traditional Gosport ferry which served the route so faithfully during its heyday. Her sale to Gosport Cruising Club for use as their headquarters in 1965 proved fruitless; a sad end to an active little craft.

One wonders what the next chapter in the history of the Gosport Ferry will be and it remains to be seen if the 'Queens' will see their 50th birthdays in service – spare parts and circumstances permitting!

*The use of the **Portsmouth Queen** and **Gosport Queen** in tandem remains a regular practice despite their senior years. Here the **Gosport Queen** approaches the temporary Endeavour Quay pontoon at Gosport in August 2011 as observed from the promenade deck of sister **Portsmouth Queen**. This operation was necessary whilst the new Gosport pontoon was installed. The newer fleet members were too large for the temporary facility. (Andrew Cooke)*

8 Expensive Doesn't Always Mean Best

by William Mayes

When one likes to try many different cruising experiences, often with less well-known companies on foreign language ships, it is important to set one's expectations at the right level. When booking a budget-priced all-inclusive cruise with a Spanish operator using a ship that has almost sunk, is 41 years old, is registered in the Marshall Islands and has been rejected by The Peaceboat Organisation, the expectation level is not high. Seeing the ship limping into Barcelona five hours late (we later learned that she had experienced engine problems and was late leaving Valencia) and leaving a trail of black smoke did nothing to raise that level.

OCEAN PEARL

Our ship for this trip was the *Ocean Pearl*, built in 1970 as the *Song of Norway* and the very first ship for the newly created Royal Caribbean Cruise Line. She was lengthened in 1978 when a new 26-metre mid section was inserted. It was interesting to walk around the ship to search for the joins, most of which are still apparent today to those who know where to look.

By 1997 the ship was too small and, following the removal of the Viking Crown Lounge, was sold to Sun Cruises (Airtours) who operated her as the *Sundream* until 2004 when that company withdrew from the operation of its own cruise ships. She passed to a Cypriot-registered company and was chartered to Caspi Cruises of Israel as the *Dream Princess*, later becoming the *Dream* in 2006. During September 2007 while alongside in Rhodes she developed a heavy list and almost sank at her berth following the failure of a ballast pump. Eventually righted, she remained in Rhodes, where in November during high winds she broke her moorings and collided with a cargo ship. Later that year she passed to the Danish Clipper group for whom she was renamed initially as the *Clipper Pearl*. On her charter to the Peaceboat Organisation in 2008, she was renamed *Clipper Pacific* but her first (and only) voyage was something of a disaster with numerous problems causing the charter to be terminated in Piraeus and the passengers transferred to the hastily chartered *Mona Lisa*. In 2009 she was again chartered to Caspi Cruises and, after a long refit in Bulgaria, took the name *Festival*. For 2010 and 2011 she has had summer charters to Happy Cruises (formerly Quail Cruises). She is managed by International Shipping Partners of Miami, who also provide the deck and engine room officers and crew.

*The happy **Ocean Pearl** in Villefranche. (William Mayes)*

The Tropicana Lounge still has many signs of its time as the My Fair Lady Lounge. (William Mayes)

The Coral Dining Room. (William Mayes)

The Piano Bar. (William Mayes)

EMBARKATION

We had deposited our heavy luggage at the terminal, conveniently adjacent to the Grand Marina Hotel where we had stayed overnight, and were advised that check-in would commence at 13.00. The ship arrived at about 12.45, but we duly turned up to check in soon after the appointed hour. That gave us our first surprise; the process was fairly slick and relatively informal, so we were on board the *Ocean Pearl* within about 20 minutes – one of my fastest embarkations ever. I suppose it helps that the ship has two embarkation ports with about 70 per cent of the passengers embarking in Valencia and the remainder in Barcelona.

A steward showed us to our Promenade Deck outside cabin, situated in the 1978 extension, the design and size of which clearly resembled that of a 1970s Scandinavian ferry. The cabin was small, the window end being almost entirely occupied by a double bed. There was a small bedside chest, a shelf and chair and two small curtain-fronted areas of hanging space, one of which contained a safe. The shower room was tiny and we later found that the water temperature was unpredictable and the pressure almost non-existent at times of peak demand. However, our steward kept the cabin spotlessly clean.

After a brief but tasty lunch in the Lido Buffet on Deck 8 (the food throughout the week was very much better than expected) it was time for a first quick tour of the ship, leading us to believe that much of the artwork and decorative panels were original. However, later in the trip, on closer inspection it was discovered that virtually all of this material dated from 1987 or 1988, so the ship must have had a major internal makeover around then.

A first drink in the Tropicana Lounge, before boat drill, was a pleasant change from the almost complete lack of any sort of bar service experienced on board the *Grand Holiday* during the previous week. On the *Ocean Pearl* there was efficient, friendly and seemingly happy table service from a variety of staff with English skills ranging from very good to almost non-existent. But the language really did not matter – it was all part of the fun and during the week I think that we only had one incorrect drink delivered.

Boat drill on the *Ocean Pearl* was also in sharp contrast with the shambolic effort (largely as a result of unruly passengers) on the *Grand Holiday*. Here one felt that in an emergency the crew and passengers would at least know where to go. For this cruise there were 920 passengers aboard, somewhat less than the ship's capacity for Happy Cruises of 1,050. Even with that number of passengers, this small ship never felt crowded. Many of the passengers were young, maybe late teens and early 20s, clearly part of school or college groups visiting historical sites and learning about other cultures. We found them to be no problem at all and were quite surprised at the way in which young Spanish people were prepared to join in with on-board activities in a way that British youngsters would not. We later learned, however, that they were a bit of a handful at night and ran riot from time to time, causing damage and inconvenience, so perhaps they are not so different from the British after all?

LAYOUT

The layout of the ship is fairly simple. Deck 6 has most of the public rooms. The Tropicana Lounge, forward, was formerly the My Fair Lady Lounge and much of the decor still evokes that image, including some wonderful glass panels depicting a day at Ascot. This room has a small stage and dance floor, above which is a very attractive convex Tiffany glass ceiling.

The cream and purple seating was initially something of a shock but we quickly became acclimatised. Interestingly, a small amount of sheer is discernable at the forward end of this room. Aft of this is the foyer leading to Coral Restaurant (formerly The King and I Dining Room) featuring a concave metal engraving that depicts the ship in Oslo, before lengthening. In the dining room itself there is still evidence of the connection to Siam, with at least three large depictions of boats from the region. Here the tables are quite closely packed, making the job of the waiters that much more difficult. Although it is possible to walk through the dining room to gain access to the after rooms, it is not encouraged. What was the card room, the former dining room extension, is now an almost clinical-looking coffee bar with a small library and Internet room off to the port side.

The last room on this deck is the former South Pacific Lounge, the main entertainment centre of the ship, now named as the Cabaret Lounge. Again there were decorative items in this attractive room that linked to the past theme.

The former Lounge of the Midnight Sun at the after end of Deck 7, in its heyday probably the best room on the ship with its panoramic sweep of windows overlooking the stern, is now something of a mixture of smaller spaces. Named the Piano Bar, it has a pleasant bar area on the port side forward, with further evidence of the ship's former identity, and the casino on the starboard side. Further aft is the Starlight Discotheque, a teenagers' area with 'trendy teenage style' seating and a table tennis table. Aft of that, in the sweep of the windows, is the dance floor.

Externally the ship was generally in good repair, and the few areas that were not up to scratch were being worked on quite thoroughly by the maintenance team, to the extent that metalwork was being taken back to bare metal before being repainted. Several much-painted handrails on external crew-only stairways where the paint was probably thicker than the metal were being cut away and replaced with new, as were many of the pipes draining water from the upper decks. The well-varnished wooden decks were also in surprisingly good condition, although there was much evidence of repair where small sections had been replaced over the years.

On the Gala night we were invited to the Captain's table, along with three other (non-Spanish) passengers. That meant that the Tapas at 17.00 was rather more welcome than usual as our dinner would not begin until some five hours later; British passengers are generally allocated to first sitting on Spanish ships, and at 20.00 that was about right for us.

On our sea day between Naples and Valencia our request to visit the

*The after deck and pool of the **Le Boreal**. (William Mayes)*

bridge had been granted and Captain Terry Konstaninidis graciously spent an hour or so with us talking ships. I suppose that it must be unusual on a typical Western Mediterranean circuit such as this (Barcelona, Villefranche, Livorno, Civitavecchia, Naples and Valencia) to get passengers who are actually interested in the ship and her history. We were also invited back for departure from Valencia, an invitation that we were delighted to accept.

Arrival in Barcelona on the final day was on time, as we had been assured by the Captain that it would be. That was fortunate, as had the ship arrived at the same time as the week before, we would have been watching our flight depart, from the after deck of the rather delightful, and charmingly crewed *Ocean Pearl*. I think that tells you that our expectations had been exceeded by a very good margin.

LE BOREAL

A cruise advertised as a 'Gastronomic Experience' on a nearly new upmarket French ship evokes thoughts of sumptuous meals and outstanding service. The reality was rather different. The *Le Boreal* entered service with Ponant Cruises in 2010. She is the first of a pair of yacht-like vessels that carries just 260 passengers. Ponant Cruises is largely owned by the containership operator CMA CGM.

We boarded the *Le Boreal* in Marseille during the morning, as the ship was due to sail at midday. We were delayed by an hour while awaiting some late arrivals and took the opportunity for lunch before sailing. This was the first disappointment as lunch (and breakfast we later found) were only available as self-service meals. We took lunch on the open deck aft of the Grill Restaurant on Deck 6. Choice was somewhat limited but what was available was good (but certainly not Gourmet). The layout of the Grill Restaurant self-service area is both confusing and congested and this was the only time that our group of six ate there.

Breakfasts and lunches in the Gastronomique Restaurant on Deck 2 did not live up to the name either. The food was adequate but no better, and the self-service style was totally out of keeping with the ambiance of the room. Sometimes dishes ran out and were not replaced and at one breakfast much of the cooked food was cold because a burner underneath the tray had either gone out or not been lit in the first place.

*The **Le Boreal** alongside in Marseille. (William Mayes)*

The red and grey theme even extends to the elegant, if slightly impractical cabins. (William Mayes)

Part of the Panoramic Lounge with the small library in the background. (William Mayes)

The Gastronomique Restaurant failed to live up to its name on this trip. (William Mayes)

We will come back to dinners later but first a brief tour of this very chic French ship. The Restaurant is at the after end of Deck 2 (Pont Le Liberté), and clearly a trick has been missed here as the stairway from the deck above could easily have been made into a 'grand entrance', whereas in reality it was more akin to descending into a car deck.

The Main Lounge on Deck 3 was called just that: not very French. However, the decks are all named after French liners of the past and this one is Pont Le Champollion. This attractive room was the venue for afternoon tea, a vocal duo in the evenings, and other minor entertainment. The colour scheme here and throughout the ship was white or pale cream and grey with splashes of red. Forward of this room is the small (and expensive) shop and the lower level of the two-deck atrium, housing the excursion desk and reception. Cabins occupy the forward parts of this deck and the two above.

The after end of Deck 4 (Pont Le Lafayette) is the location for the Theatre, and it was here that our group received a 'welcome on board' talk from the Captain. Although the cruises on this ship are sold as being bi-lingual, with just the six English speakers on board, this cruise was conducted almost entirely in French.

Above the Theatre, on Pont Le Normandie, is the fitness area, a part of the ship that did not detain us for long. Deck 6 is named Pont Le France and has the grill aft and the Panoramic Lounge, actually the best room on the ship, at the forward end with cabins between the two. Pont Le France, above, has the Open-Air Bar, sundeck and stowage area for the ship's Zodiacs.

So, to dinner; certainly a gastronomic extravaganza, but perhaps not quite what we had expected. Each evening there was a gastronomic event in the Theatre, usually involving that evening's Michelin Starred or Award Winning chef. We were expected to be in the Restaurant at a set time, but timing was not their strongpoint and dinner was served variously 30 minutes to over an hour late. Then we had to endure a detailed description for each course in French from the chef as to how the elements of the meal had bonded with the earth and how they now sat together in perfect harmony. As each course had its matching wine, the award-winning Sommelier also had to describe each wine in great detail. A three- or four-course dinner generally took up to three hours to complete and as the portions were really quite small there was no sensation of being remotely full at the end of it. That said, most of what was offered was interesting, tasty and well presented, but generally fairly uninspiring. One of the desserts closely resembled one we had eaten on the ferry *Pont-Aven*.

Had our expectations been met? Well, the ship was lovely, and the cabins were of a good size, even if some of the features were impractical or just odd. The public rooms were attractive and inviting and the staff exceptional. But, the whole trip was let down by the food and the elaborate theatre at dinner. So, no this one failed to meet our expectations. I would like to try Ponant Cruises again, but on a regular cruise.

9 The Manxman Project
by Adrian Sweeney

EARLY EFFORTS

It seems amazing to think now but the *Manxman* Project, the efforts to save the ex-Isle of Man Steam Packet Company steamer *Manxman* for future generations to enjoy and appreciate, started off, albeit in embryonic form, at the end of the last century!

The first tentative, informal efforts came as a result of a conversation between the late John Coates and myself as we were setting in motion the plans for 'Ships of Mann' Magazine in mid-1999. We quite simply decided that we needed a focus and a cause and trying to save the *Manxman* seemed to be the ideal way forward. Looking back now, 12 years later, it all seems such a naïve thing to try and do! We really had little idea, at that time, of the complexities involved in pursuing a project of this size in financial, commercial or even political terms and perhaps it is as well that we didn't, otherwise the attempted preservation of the *Manxman* might have been over before it began.

Unbeknown to us, however, another keen maritime enthusiast was also taking an interest in the fate of the *Manxman* and was trying to chart a similar course to ourselves. He was making contacts with people, organisations and authorities he thought might be interested in helping to save this wonderful example of our maritime heritage. He was of course, later to become our great friend and colleague on the *Manxman* Project, Bill Ogle.

In late October 1999 John Coates rang the Pallion Shipyard in Sunderland and asked to speak to someone about the *Manxman*. He was put through to the Manager of the yard, Peter Callaghan, and a discussion ensued about the possibility of liberating the ship from the banks of the River Wear. Arrangements were made for John and myself to visit the ship on the 3rd November. It was, indeed, not too many weeks beforehand that the *Manxman* had 'sprung a leak' and was only just rescued from capsizing by the efforts of the staff at Pallion and the local fire brigade.

Our meeting with the people at Pallion was very successful despite the fact that they probably were wondering which institution we had been given day release from! Over three hours of discussions were held with Peter Callaghan and his colleague, Bob Pearson of Magpie Marine, about

*The **Manxman** returns to Llandudno Pier after a cruise along the North Wales Coast towards Anglesey on 3rd September 1978. (Andrew King)*

the condition of the vessel, our plans for her future, time scale and all the other elements that have to be brought together on this sort of proposed project. Later we were given free and full access to the ship herself, which of course at this time was outside on the Pallion Wharf and still afloat. Walking the decks once more of this maritime legend was indeed a special moment for us both.

However, all these formative efforts to secure the future of the ship met with little success. Funding was, of course, the key and our initial efforts in this direction were centred on the Isle of Man although we found out later that Bill was focusing on the Merseyside area. The problem was that we were working in isolation and although a couple of wealthy Manx entrepreneurs expressed great interest in the project, that is as far as it went. Great interest, sadly, does not mean financial support and so after 12 months of hard work we had to inform Pallion that we had not had the success we had hoped for and we would have to regroup and think again. Pallion, for their part, realised there was great interest in saving the ship and so all thoughts of sending her for scrap were put on hold.

A view of the shelter deck aft, showing the famous bench-style seating, looking towards the stern on the port side. (Andrew King)

MANXMAN STEAMSHIP COMPANY

It was a chance telephone call from a Martin Hill in the spring of 2002 which re-awakened our interest in reviving the *Manxman* Project. Martin was a great enthusiast of ship preservation and although he was not to be a member of the project team for very long, he did perform one invaluable service – he acted as a catalyst to bring people of like mind together.

Thus it was arranged that John Coates and myself, Bill Ogle, Martin and Chris Brindle met together in June 2002 at a Knowsley hotel and after several hours of fruitful talks decided to set up the *Manxman* Steamship Company Limited. This new Company would take over and pull together all the work that had been done in isolation concerning the saving of the *Manxman*. It was first necessary to formulate a Company Structure that was appropriate for the future development of the project and thus the Company was immediately registered at Companies House as a 'Company Limited by Guarantee' and soon afterwards was registered at the Charity Commission as Charity Number 1100247.

It is perhaps appropriate at this stage to pay tribute to the numerous trustees of the Company who worked so hard over the years in trying to secure a future for the old Manx steamer. Of the original team members John Coates was the first chairman of the project and worked incredibly hard on its behalf. Poor health dogged John's efforts in the end and sadly he tragically passed away in May 2004. Bill Ogle was Company Secretary at the beginning and on John's passing took over the role of Chairman, a position he held until the end of the Project. It is impossible in a short article such as this to fully do justice to the tremendous amount of sheer hard work that Bill put into the project, both publicly and behind the scenes but it is suffice to say, without Bill, the progress that was made would have been far less. Chris Brindle took over the IT sector of the Company, setting up websites and systems, and maintaining them over a number of years to a very high standard. As time went on we welcomed new trustees to our project. These included Nigel Hughes, whose infectious enthusiasm was limitless and who brought past experience in the world of ship preservation as well as much-needed skills in the world of public relations and catering management, which would have been vital to the running of the preserved ship if she was going to earn her keep. He also set up and co-ordinated the support group, 'Friends of the *Manxman*' which did so much to raise funds and involve huge numbers of ordinary enthusiasts in the progress of the project; his value can never be underestimated. Other trustees who we welcomed on board

included Peter Elson of the 'Liverpool Daily Post', a passionate advocate of Merseyside's maritime heritage, Gordon McLeod, a preservation enthusiast whose wise counsel was often sought, Dave Hulse of the union GMB, whose support of the project was deeply appreciated, Ian McGregor from Scotland, who brought to the project a wide knowledge of local government funding priorities, Brian Johnson, the former Chief Engineer of the *Manxman* herself and who had just retired from the position of Engineering Superintendent of the Isle of Man Steam Packet Company, and Mrs Audrey Mansell of Port St Mary, Isle of Man, the daughter of the *Manxman*'s first captain, the legendary 'Ginger' Bridson. It can be thus be appreciated that the team which was involved with Project *Manxman* came from a wide variety of backgrounds with a very wide range of appropriate skills needed to take it forward.

The sheer ambition of the *Manxman* Project not only needed its support group, 'Friends of the *Manxman*' but also individual patrons and supporters of status and influence. We were lucky enough to have the support of three such people throughout the life of the project, Lord Alton, the Right Honourable Frank Field, MP and the Lieutenant Governor of the Isle of Man, Air Marshall Ian MacFadyen. We were fortunate also to have the full support of the present day Isle of Man Steam Packet Company and its then Managing Director, Captain Hamish Ross and the then Marine Superintendent Captain Peter Corrin, himself the last skipper of the *Manxman*, who went out of their way to make it easy for us to charter the *Lady of Mann* three times for Round the Island Cruises and who made available to us any technical help and support that we required.

PROJECT OBJECTIVES

So, what exactly were the aims and objectives of the project? Put simply, the main aim was to bring the ship back to her birthplace at Birkenhead. There she would be sympathetically restored to her original condition or as much as it was possible to do so but of course the ship had to 'earn a living' and thus certain areas of the ship would have been restored with that in mind. The actual restoration of the ship was seen as an opportunity for apprentices from the Cammell Laird Foundation to learn skills new to them but traditional in their heritage, skills which were being lost but in the longer term would be vital to revive and restore. Thus local employment and skills revival were seen as a very important factor, especially during the phases of restoration, but also important for the ongoing maintenance of

*The boat deck of the **Manxman** looking forward on 29th July 2008 in the Pallion dry dock. Although all the original lifeboats are still in place this part of the ship was much altered during her days as a nightclub in Preston. (Adrian Sweeney)*

*A view from the flying bridge of the **Manxman** looking aft on the starboard side, inside the Pallion dry dock on 3rd June 2010. From this position the ship was often navigated especially when going astern out of Douglas or into Fleetwood. (Adrian Sweeney)*

The **Manxman** sails for the first time for many years as she is moved from the Pallion Wharf to the indoor dry dock at Pallion Shipyard for what was hoped to be the first stage of the restoration project, on 25th September 2003. (Adrian Sweeney)

A view of the **Manxman**, taken from the opposite side of the River Wear, resting at her berth at the Pallion Wharf, Sunderland on 3rd November 1999. She had been in this position since arriving at the Pallion Shipyard from Hull on 12th December 1997. (Adrian Sweeney)

The **Manxman** at her berth on the Pallion Wharf taken on 3rd November 1999. Note the cut away at the bow, which was a legacy of her time at Hull when her owners had tried to squeeze her into a dry dock that was not quite big enough! (Adrian Sweeney)

the preserved ship.

So, once restored, what would the *Manxman* have offered to the local community and as a visitor attraction? It was thought that, although the *Manxman* could have survived as a stand alone attraction, it would have been more viable if she had been part of a 'maritime park' at Birkenhead, perhaps co-ordinating her attractions with the Historic Warships and other preservation projects within the area. The collapse of the Historic Warships at Birkenhead while Project *Manxman* was in full swing sadly curtailed that idea, and indeed did much damage to the *Manxman* Project itself in terms of long-term viability.

The ship herself would have had several different functions as a static exhibit and attraction, although it must be pointed out that although it was thought unlikely the ship would ever 'steam' again, the Company decided to keep in the engines in a high state of preservation 'just in case'!

One of the most important functions of the vessel would have been as an educational resource for the schools of the local area and beyond. Plans were put in place for a classroom to be developed in one of the former lounges and from there various educational projects could have been developed. Studies of social history and how people lived in the 1940s and 50s were high on the agenda – both at work and at play – where working people went on their holidays and how they got there would have seen the original passenger areas which had been restored play a major role in this particular enlightenment of modern children. Various aspects of engineering, using the engine room of the ship would also have had a significant role to play.

Various exhibitions, both permanent and temporary were seen as an important role for the ship. For example, a TT history museum was actively considered as well as using the ship as a focal point for the Manx tourist industry, both past and present.

The *Manxman* was also seen as a high-class resource for functions and meetings, both corporate and private. It was the intention to restore the former first class restaurant to its former silver service glory and make it the centrepiece for wedding celebrations, private dinners and corporate hospitality. To supplement the corporate aspect of the plans, it was intended to convert some areas of the ship to modern functioning meeting rooms where companies could hold meetings in unusual and pleasant surroundings.

And of course, the ship was intended to be a visitor centre for the general public who could come aboard, have a pleasant learning experience visiting an historic ship, have a meal in one of the restaurants or just a snack from one of the restored kiosks and hopefully buy some souvenirs from one of the well-stocked retail outlets!

PROJECT PROGRESS
HISTORIC VESSELS REGISTER

The *Manxman* Project was a serious attempt to preserve and restore the historic vessel and there were many successes and achievements along the way. The trustees realised early on that if the project was to have any chance of success then it was essential to get the old ship recognised as a serious example of maritime heritage. Therefore we applied to the Historic Vessels Register to have the *Manxman* registered and we were successful not only in adding her to the register but also our arguments about her heritage were so convincing that she was, after only a short time, put on to the Designated List, which is the second highest category on the register. The highest sector is the Core List, which includes ships such as the *Mary Rose* and *Cutty Sark* and it was towards including the *Manxman* on the Core List that the Project

*A view of the fo'c'sle of the **Manxman** looking aft taken from the forepeak on 29th July 2008. The anchor chains and machinery are still in place and more or less intact. This of course was a favourite place for passengers once the ship was at sea. (Adrian Sweeney)*

*The twin propellers and rudder of the **Manxman** have not turned for nearly 30 years but this view taken on 3rd June 2010 in the dry dock at Pallion Shipyard shows that they are still intact and in good condition. (Adrian Sweeney)*

team was working, right up to the end.

Heritage Lottery Fund and Surveys

It was always envisaged that the bulk of the funding needed to save the *Manxman* would have to come from the Heritage Lottery Fund. The project was successful in its first application for funds, which was in the form of a large Development Grant. This enabled the project to embark on a number of essential surveys which were vital to its future progress.

The surveys included a full hull condition survey done in April 2003, which of course was essential to determine the true condition of a hull which had been in the water since 1982. The survey was also essential for any future towing of the ship away from Sunderland. Inevitably the hull survey was thorough and complex but basically stated that although there would have to be repairs and modifications in certain areas, the ship was in reasonably sound condition and would probably receive permission from the Maritime and Coastguard Agency (MCA) for her tow to the Mersey.

The Trustees of the Project were constantly aware that once the *Manxman* returned to the Mersey, once she was restored, she would have to earn a living. Therefore an Audience Development Research Report was commissioned from L&R Consulting in August 2003. This extremely detailed report was very upbeat about the potential of the ship as a day visitor attraction, an educational resource, a corporate venue and an events venue – in other words, the plans that the Project had formulated were very feasible, workable and had a great chance of success.

Other detailed surveys carried out at around this time included an asbestos removal survey provided by Malrod Insulations Limited, an insurance survey together with a survey to upgrade the fire and security systems on the vessel. These two latter surveys were included in a full report from North Western Shiprepairers and Shipbuilders, Birkenhead in January 2004, and it also contained updates to work which would be needed to strip the ship of her internal nightclub fittings ready for full restoration and also the fitting of a lift to all decks so that the ship could comply with all disabled access legislation.

Early in 2004 a comprehensive Business Plan was formulated and was updated and reviewed constantly by the Trustees as time went on and a Commercial Development Plan was also produced. The formulation of vital policy documents also went on apace including the areas of Access, Acquisitions, Conservation, Education, Equal Opportunities (including a Code of Practice), and a Training Policy. The Trustees were working constantly to make sure no angles were left uncovered as the project progressed.

DRY DOCKING

On 25th September 2003, the *Manxman* was moved from her river berth into the covered dry dock at Pallion Shipyard – a very significant date in the history of the project. It was only a 'sailing' of a few hundred metres but it was the first time the ship had moved since she had arrived on the Wear many years before. Once in dry dock, work began on some preliminary restoration work, including some much-needed hull re-plating and the restoration of the ship's bow, part of which had been cut away to facilitate her berthing at Hull in the mid-1990s.

NATIONAL LOTTERY APPLICATION AND FURTHER PROGRESS

In April 2004 the Project was ready to submit its main application for substantial Heritage Lottery funding. Meanwhile, as we were waiting for the response from the Lottery, further substantial progress was made.

Negotiations were finally concluded with the Mersey Docks and Harbour Company for a permanent berth for the ship once she was returned to the Mersey. These negotiations had been long and complex as the Harbour Company wanted to make sure the ship was safe to enter the Mersey and the dock system and they needed guarantees that the ongoing safety of the ship was paramount and that the business plans of the Project were robust enough to guarantee the financial security of the ship and project.

Long and ultimately fruitful negotiations were also held with the Laird Foundation in Birkenhead for the *Manxman* to have her restoration in the Number 4 dry dock at Birkenhead. While undergoing this restoration the ship would become a focus for the training of shipyard apprentices not only in modern techniques but also in the traditional shipyard crafts common in the yards of Cammell Laird in the 1950s but now no longer used over 50 years later.

THE FIRST SETBACK

Perhaps this sub-title should read the first 'major' setback as it was the first serious body blow to the success of the project. The Heritage Lottery declined our application for major funding. Although they had small concerns in a number of areas, the main reason for the rejection was the lack of Local Authority support for the project which they thought was vital for its long-term success. So although it was not a matter of 'back to the drawing board', much work needed to be done to bring on board the various Local Authorities of Merseyside and beyond. The difficulty was, that we had been trying to do this since the project began, and although many meetings had taken place with both Local Authorities individually and with Local Authority groupings, none of them were prepared to make any financial commitment to the ship and her future. We had plenty of moral support, loads of good wishes, plenty of promises of future goodwill, but no commitment which would satisfy the Heritage Lottery. And over the next few years, despite prolonged negotiations with them all, that is how it stayed. There was one slight ripple of hope from Liverpool City Council in the run up to the 2008 European City of Culture when a large sum of money was supposedly match funded but sadly this came to nothing as well, despite the continued efforts of the project team.

The project was also beginning to find it more and more difficult to attract private investors as well, especially after the rejection by the Heritage Lottery. Everybody thought the project was a fantastic idea, ambitious and exciting, thoroughly worthwhile, but no-one, from wealthy individuals to corporate organisations were prepared to back the scheme with cash! Plenty of promises were forthcoming but most of these turned out to be empty ones.

CARRY ON REGARDLESS ...

Despite all the difficulties and mounting setbacks, the *Manxman* Steamship Company continued to further the progress of the project. In 2003, 2004 and 2005 the *Lady of Mann* was chartered from the Isle of Man Steam Packet Company for a Round the Island Cruise. All three of these cruises were fantastically supported by the general public of the Isle of Man and were all highly successful. It showed that the support for the project was firm at grass roots level if not in the upper echelons of government and business.

On 8th February 2005 the project celebrated the 50th Anniversary of the launching of the *Manxman* with a service in the church of Our Lady and St Nicholas at the Pier Head Liverpool, accompanied by a peel of bells from the Anglican Cathedral. Later in the morning the Mersey ferry, *Royal Iris*,

*The final resting place of the steamer **Manxman**? The classic lines of this wonderful steamer are still well in evidence as she awaits her fate in the Pallion dry dock on 3rd June 2010. An everlasting testament perhaps to the apathetic and uncaring attitude in which the maritime heritage of the United Kingdom is held. (Adrian Sweeney)*

flying the name pennant of the *Manxman* and the house flag of the *Manxman* Steamship Company sailed past the slipway at Cammell Laird at precisely 11.15, fifty years ago to the minute when the *Manxman* was launched.

Meanwhile further progress was made when IWC Media proposed a partnership with the project for a series of TV restoration programmes charting the course of the restoration of this historic ship. However, as progress began to stall and the momentum began to slip away, this partnership eventually came to nothing.

THE SECOND SETBACK AND THE END

In January 2006 the Historic Warship Collection at Birkenhead went into liquidation and ceased trading. The trustees at the *Manxman* Project viewed this development with alarm as there had been tentative plans for the two projects to work collaboratively. However, the hard work went on, the trustees continuing to make progress on a revised Heritage Lottery bid, as well as discussing and negotiating with local government and corporate organisations for funding and support.

And then in 2007 came the second major and ultimately fatal setback. Peel Ports, who had taken over Mersey Docks and Harbour Company previously, withdrew the offer of the berth for the *Manxman*, citing that the project did not fit into their plans for the future of the Birkenhead Dock estate. And that was that. Despite prolonged lobbying from not only the trustees of the project but also from a number of high profile supporters, Peel Ports would not change their minds. The *Manxman* no longer had a berth and this was the killer blow. If the project could not bring the ship back to the Mersey all hope of future funding was lost. The Local Authorities declined to support the trustees in their efforts to change the mind of Peel Ports and they melted away. Without a berth at Birkenhead the

charity could no longer meet its charitable obligations and all progress came to a shuddering halt. Support for the project faded away and future funding streams dried up.

Meanwhile the ship remained in the dry dock at Pallion, Sunderland, rapidly deteriorating as she lay on the blocks year after year. During 2010 it had become obvious that the ship could not be saved, not only because of the immovable obstacle put in the project's way by Peel Ports but also because the condition of the ship was now such that it would have cost many millions of pounds more than had been envisaged as recently as 2007. All that remained was for Pallion to make the decision to break the old ship up, a decision, much to their credit, they kept putting off every time there was only the slightest glimmer of hope. Sadly all glimmers have now been absorbed by the gloom.

EPILOGUE

When we started the *Manxman* Project we always realised that the odds were against us. What we wanted to do to the ship should have been done in 1982 when she was withdrawn from service – we were over 20 years too late. However, the project, as hopefully can be seen from this account of events was a serious and very professional attempt to save and restore a vital part of the maritime and engineering history of our nation. The *Manxman* Steamship Company, sadly, failed to persuade enough of the organisations, both public and private, who mattered, that the restored *Manxman* would be a fantastic national and local maritime icon.

Perhaps it was a case of knowing the cost of everything and the value of nothing…

Round Britain Cruise

by Miles Cowsill

The *Black Watch* was built in 1972, as the first of a trio of purpose-built luxury cruise ships for worldwide service for Royal Viking Line. When delivered by Wartsila of Helsinki as the *Royal Viking Star*, she introduced new and impressive standards for the cruise industry. As built she was 21,847 gross tons and could carry 539 passengers in luxurious surroundings. Eleven years later, she was lengthened by Schichau Seebeckwerft in Bremerhaven to give her an increased passenger capacity of 758. In 1988 she was transferred to Kloster Cruise, the new owners of Royal Viking Line, and three years later was given the name *Westward*. Ten years later, she was transferred within the Group to Royal Cruise Line and she was renamed the *Star Odyssey*. Fred. Olsen purchased her in 1996 and following a refit she entered service as the *Black Watch*. In 2005 she underwent a major refit, including replacement of her engines. Today, she operates with a passenger certificate of 902 passengers who are served by 330 crew.

The *Black Watch* undertakes a variety of cruises throughout her season with Fred. Olsen and one of the most popular of her summer cruises is her Round Britain cruise, which this year took in Guernsey, Dublin, Greenock, Bangor (Northern Ireland), Tobermory and Orkney, commencing and finishing at Dover.

There are not many opportunities offered by cruise companies to take in a Round Britain cruise of this type and when invited by the company to travel on this cruise it was something that I could not resist, being so interested in the geography of the British Isles. Our departure on the first leg of the cruise allowed for a late afternoon sailing from Dover with an early morning arrival in St Peter Port the next day. The weather as we left Dover was very inclement but the domineering white cliffs of the Kentish coast and Dover Castle made for a fine departure from this important port, which for so many years has been the gateway to continental Europe. As the ship made her way down the coast, passengers were exploring ship and exchanging reminiscences with fellow passengers, many of whom had travelled on the ship previously.

Like most cruise ships, there are two sittings for dinner on board, one at 18.15 and the second at 20.30, both of which are served in the Glentanar Restaurant. The vessel has three main bars, one midships on Deck 6, the Piper's Bar, which features memorabilia from the Black Watch Regiment, which the ship has had close associations with during over the years. At the aft on Deck 6 is the Marquee Bar, which also serves the poolside area

*The **Black Watch** heads away from St Peter Port for Dublin during her 'Round Britain Cruise'. (Tony Rive)*

The immaculately maintained decks of the **Black Watch** with the island of
Herm in the background. (Miles Cowsill)

RESCUE BOAT STATION 2

The **SeaFrance Moliere** *swings off her berth at Dover as the* **Black Watch** *moves out of the port on the start of her Round Britain cruise. (Miles Cowsill)*

P&O Ferries' **Norbank** *dwarfs the row of Guinness tankers awaiting transportation across the Irish Sea to Liverpool. In spite of Guinness brewing in the UK, the original factory plays an important role in keeping drinkers happy in Britain. (Miles Cowsill)*

around the various swimming facilities offered on this deck. The other main bar on board the ship is in the Observatory Lounge, located on Deck 9, which offers excellent views forward. This bar also doubles up for the serving of afternoon teas when the ship is at sea and not visiting a port.

The *Black Watch* offers various other passenger areas for the comfort of her guests, including the Lido Lounge, where morning coffee and afternoon tea is served, the Explorers Library, internet centre, card room and casino on Lido Deck. The Braemar Room allows passengers to listen to a variety of music from the on-board pianist throughout the day, where there is another small bar. The largest passenger room on board the *Black Watch* is the Neptune Lounge, which at most times of the day offers entertainment for passengers and in the evening is the venue for the gala entertainment.

The vessel over the years has been gradually improved by Fred. Olsen over the years and improvements to the cabin accommodation are still undergoing with further work being undertaken to the cabins located on Decks 3, 4 and 5 this year. The company hope to operate the ship for a further ten years, when she will be a grand lady of some 40 years of age.

The main shopping facilities, run by Harding Brothers, are located on Deck 5 and offer a wide range of shopping for passengers, all very realistically priced in the writer's view. On Deck 3 is the Marina Theatre, which today is the on-board cinema for the ship.

THE CRUISE TO GUERNSEY

After a very pleasant dinner in the Glentanar Restaurant, our party, which included journalists from the Daily & Sunday Telegraph and various other media, took evening drinks in the Observatory Lounge as the Isle of Wight disappeared into the twilight.

Our next day arrival at St Peter Port was on schedule and all passengers were transferred by launch into the heart of the Victorian port. A day in St Peter Port is still as fascinating as ever with the many little ferries leaving the harbour for Herm and Sark at all times of the day, and of course the Condor vessels are regular ships coming into St Peter Port from Weymouth, Poole and St Helier. As we arrived at St Peter Port, the *Commodore Goodwill* had just left on her early morning arrival with her essential goods for the island and was en route to St Helier and St Malo on her special Saturday run to France. Guernsey benefits from over 100 calls on average each year in stark contrast to Jersey, which only has a few.

St Peter Port has become a very popular destination for cruise liners in recent years, especially as it is still a duty-free state, as it is not a member of the EU. Some of the largest liners in the world come to St Peter Port and anchor in the Little Russell between Guernsey and Herm, which at most times gives protection from the westerly winds. In certain weather conditions passengers can be disappointed as the swell in the Little Russell is too much to tender passengers ashore.

After an enjoyable day in St Peter Port, the *Black Watch* departed at 17.30 for Dublin. Already the Captain Terje Ulset had indicated that the weather was to deteriorate from a lovely sunny day, which all on board had enjoyed, to torrential rain and winds with a deep low coming in over Ireland and the Irish Sea. On this front the Captain did not let us down as the next morning the decks of the *Black Watch* offered only torrential rain and mist as we headed across the British Channel to the coast of Pembrokeshire, which would have, had the weather been in our favour, given us outstanding views of the rugged coast of West Wales and the islands of Skomer and Skokholm. The majority of the passengers were confined to the inside of the vessel for most of the day since the rain persisted as we moved along the Welsh coast

*The **Condor Vitesse** pushes away from St. Peter Port en route to Poole. Condor Ferries with their three fast craft and two conventional ships are a regular scene off the Guernsey port. (Miles Cowsill)*

*Looking aft on the **Black Watch** with the distinctive funnel of the vessel. (Miles Cowsill)*

*The **Black Watch** has a wealth of outdoor decks: This view shows the swimming pool area at the stern. (Miles Cowsill)*

An early morning arrival at Dublin allowed those on the 'Round Britain Cruise' the sight of Irish Ferries' **Ulysses** having just arrived from Holyhead on her overnight sailing. (Miles Cowsill)

Princess Cruises' giant cruise vessel the **Crown Princess** dwarfs the **Black Watch** as she arrives at Dublin Port. (Miles Cowsill)

P&O Ferries' two freight ships at Dublin, the **Norbank** and **European Endeavour** are pictured on their Monday's layover at the Irish port with the **Crown Princess** behind them. (Miles Cowsill)

to the Lleyn Peninsula. The more hardy of us did take in a walk around the decks in the latter part of the afternoon as the torrential rain eased off into a laden Welsh wet mist.

IRELAND & SCOTLAND

The next day, the low had moved away from the British Isles and high pressure was moving in, so much so that our arrival in Dublin allowed for brilliant sunshine. After picking up the pilot off Kish lighthouse, the *Black Watch* manoeuvred passed the recently arrived *Ulysses* from Holyhead and the *Stena Adventurer*. The cruise berth, which the *Black Watch* was to use this day, required two tugs to swing the vessel astern onto berth. As we made fast, the massive Princess Cruises' *Crown Princess*, was making her way up the River Liffey with her 3,000 passengers on board. It was interesting that most of my fellow passengers were remarking to each other that they had no desire to travel on such a ship with such a great passenger capacity and much preferred the friendly surroundings of the *Black Watch*.

Various tours were offered around Dublin City, including trips to the Guinness factory and to Phoenix Park. After sampling a very good tour laid on by Fred. Olsen around Dublin City, I retired to one of the local pubs for a couple of pints of Guinness and a hearty Irish lunch. Our evening departure from Dublin was at 18.00 and as we made our way up the Liffey, the *Stena Adventurer* was berthing again, having done a round trip to Holyhead whilst we were enjoying Dublin. The *Ulysses* also was berthing at the port having done likewise. The southern Irish coast slipped away in the mist after an hour but the climatic conditions radically changed around 22.00, and passengers were able to take in the Mourne Mountains of Northern Ireland to the port side of the ship and the Isle of Man to the starboard side, which was basked in the evening light. The Mull of Galloway also became visible in the late evening light after an hour, and then later Ailsa Craig could also be seen at the head of the Firth of Clyde as midnight approached.

Our arrival at Greenock was again on time and various sizes of coaches were on the quayside to take passengers around the highlights of the Clyde and Loch Lomond. My trip allowed for a visit to Loch Lomond, which I had not visited before, and then back to Hunters Quay to catch Western Ferries' ferry service to Greenock to allow passengers to take their lunch on board the *Black Watch*. For those less inclined to look after their stomachs, I then embarked on the train with a sandwich from Tesco for Wemyss Bay so I could do a round trip on Caledonian MacBrayne's *Argyle* and *Bute* to Rothesay. The train service slightly let me down on my return and I was the last passenger to board the *Black Watch* that evening with ten minutes to spare before her departure at 20.30. Our departure from Greenock took in the three of the four Western Ferries' ferries working hard between Greenock and Hunters Quay and soon the distinctive profile of Arran could be seen as the sun set behind it.

Our journey from Greenock to Bangor was some 92 nautical miles and the visit to this Irish port was the first of its kind for Fred. Olsen. Passengers were tendered from the protected bay of Bangor for various trips around Ulster.

WESTERN ISLES

The next part of the cruise had great significance and interest for me as it took in the Western Isles of Scotland, which is one of my favourite locations in the world. We pulled anchor at Bangor at 18.00 and set sail across Belfast Loch, taking in the Antrim coast and Rathlin Island, and the Mull of Kintyre as we made our way up the North Channel between

The **Black Watch** *heads out of Dublin Bay with the distinctive Wicklow Mountains behind. (Miles Cowsill)*

Looking forward from the stern on the promenade deck on the **Black Watch.** *(Miles Cowsill)*

Western Ferries' **Sound of Scarba** *arrives at McInroy's Point (Gourock) on one of her regular sailings across the Clyde. (Miles Cowsill)*

The **Black Watch** *at anchor off the pretty village of Tobermory, Mull. Most passengers disembarked from the vessel on her visit here to allow various trips to the island of Mull, including many wildlife boat trips. (Miles Cowsill)*

Scotland and Ireland. As we passed Larne, the *European Mariner* headed across us at our stern in her last few days in service on the Troon route. The late evening sun allowed us to take in the islands of Islay and the distinctive Papas of Jura. With the very long evenings and early mornings in this part of Scotland, it does not go dark until nearly midnight when there are crystal clear skies, and then the sun is on the horizon some three hours later.

Next morning we were at anchor at Tobermory. Passengers again were tendered from the ship to the pretty harbour with its pretty coloured cottages around the quayside. Various trips again were offered but for me I took the bird and sea cruise out to Ardmore Point. Our early afternoon departure from Tobermory coincided with the *Lord of the Isles* coming up the Sound of Mull outward bound from Oban to Barra. As we made our way out of the Sound, the *Lord of the Isles* took a slightly different course from us as she passed the lighthouse at Ardnamurchan Point. Soon the distinctive looking islands of Muck, Eigg, Rhum and Canna could be seen to the northwest. The Atlantic swell was now very evident as we headed out to sea and the little *Lord of the Isles*, in spite of her size, made ease of her course as we did. About two hours after passing Canna, the outer islands of the Hebrides could be easily seen to the west, as well as the dominating mountains on Skye to the east. Despite a beautiful sunny evening there were very few passengers like myself who took in this distinctive geographical scenery, the majority was more inclined to be holding up the bar, eating or playing bingo. Again, the late evening light allowed us to take in all these islands of Western Scotland and by 12.15 we were passing the northern point of the Isle of Lewis, Port Nis.

ORKNEY & HOME

The next morning was greeted again by outstanding weather as the *Black Watch* made her way along the Pentland Firth, passing Brough Ness (South Ronaldsay) on our way to Mull Head into the port of Hatston, near Kirkwall. For ferry lovers, Kirkwall offers a wide range of local ferries serving the outer islands of Orkney. Kirkwall itself has its own distinctive flavour and charm with the outstanding cathedral of St Magnus. Our early evening departure from Kirkwall allowed a full day at sea on the Saturday on our 547 nautical mile trip back to Dover. Soon the islands of Orkney had disappeared and as we headed away, mainland Scotland could be seen. The high pressure, which had been dominant during the last three days, slipped away from the British Isles and the next day dull skies with occasional rain greeted us as we headed down the east coast down the North Sea.

A visit to the bridge the next day to meet the captain and his fellow officers gave me a little more insight into this 'grand lady' of the cruise fleet. Fred. Olsen has spent a lot of money on the ship during their ownership and continues to do so. The *Black Watch* is well cared for by her crew and throughout all the public areas the ship was in outstanding order. The key positions on board are run by Norwegian and British personnel, while the other staffing are mostly from the Philippines, who work a nine-month contract in most cases.

During this ten-day cruise I gathered from the head chef on board some of the outstanding amounts of food that had been consumed during the cruise: over 620 litres of whipped cream, 2,500 litres of milk, 2.8 tonnes of vegetables and a combination of 2.2 tonnes of meat and poultry. It was time to diet on our arrival in Dover on the Sunday morning after a very comfortable, interesting and successful trip around Britain with a total distance of 1,825 nautical miles in all.

*Caledonian MacBrayne's **Loch Linnhe** outward bound from Tobermory with Ardmore Point lighthouse in the background, which dominates the entrance to the Sound of Mull. (Miles Cowsill)*

*Caledonian MacBrayne's **Lord of the Isles** outward bound from Oban to the Outer Hebrides. (Miles Cowsill)*

*Orkney Isles' ferry **Varagen** outward bound from Kirkwall on her evening sailing to Westray. (Miles Cowsill)*

11 Classic Liners of the Past from FotoFlite
by John Hendy

As someone born shortly after the end of World War II and living at Dover, I was fortunate to have seen many of these ships passing through the English Channel en route to their far-flung destinations. It has always been my impression that it is the ships of one's youth that perhaps linger in the memory rather longer than the box-like ships of today.

This selection from the FotoFlite archive is entirely my own and what a treasure trove that precious collection is! During those rather more carefree days, when aircraft pilots faced fewer restrictions, bridge level fly-pasts were frequent in the right conditions and without doubt the intrepid photographers captured some absolute gems. Ship designers do not intend to have their creations viewed from above - we see them from the land or from another ship and, in my personal view, the lower the angle the better the result.

The ships and the period that they represented have long since gone, killed off by the advent of the jet aircraft so that by the time I saw them, they were mostly in the twilight of their careers. The photographs cover a wide range of vessels from the tiny *Falstria* (once, with her fleet companions, a regular visitor to Dover at which time the local tender *Delphinus* would be activated to service her in the outer harbour) to the mighty *Liberte* which I was never fortunate enough to see. Greek Line's *Arkadia* always seemed to be passing Dover at the same time that I was walking home from school and became a regular sight while the *Hanseatic* was only spotted once. It was a rather wild day in the Dover Strait as she

passed serenely through, spray breaking over her bow and forward superstructure. For a ship which was originally built to cross the Pacific Ocean, such distractions were nothing and she swept majestically by into the North Sea.

On a first visit to Southampton in about 1956, I witnessed the departure of United States Line's *America* while ten years later, during the seamen's strike, so many wonderful ships were laid up during this unique gathering of all that was good and great within the assembled fleets of British liners. It was a sight that could never be repeated as within such a brief period, many of these splendid ships, which had seemed to occupy such a permanent place in our everyday lives, had sailed away to be broken up in the Far East.

The writing was already on the wall during the mid-60s and some operators usefully extended the careers of elderly ships by offering cruises. I clearly remember standing at the end of Ryde Pier one still and sunny day during the early 1970s and watching the ancient *Queen Frederica* outward bound from Southampton. Her pall of thick, black smoke stretched way back in the direction of Cowes as she carefully picked her way through the myriad of yachts busying themselves in the eastern Solent.

For me it was a realisation that within just a few years, the *Queen Frederica* and the many like her, of which the following are representative, would soon pass into history.

Orient Line's **Orsova** *is seen arriving at Tilbury possibly in preparation for her maiden voyage to Sydney in March 1954. The two-funnelled steamer is P&O's* **Maloja** *of 1923 which had completed her final voyage from Australia that January before passing for scrap in April that year. Other liners present are Orient Line's* **Orion** *(top) and one of the twin P&O 'Strath' sisters* **Strathmore** *or* **Stratheden** *while the same company's* **Chusan** *is seen on the extreme right in dry dock.*

*The Royal Mail liner **Andes** was built by Harland & Wolff in 1939 although did not enter service on the company's South American services until January 1948. At the end of the war she returned the Norwegian Government after its exile. Towards the end of her career and following a refit during winter 1959/60, she was engaged solely in cruising. Retired from service in 1971, she was broken up at Ghent.*

*Greek Line's **Arkadia** dated from 1933 when she was built as the **Monarch of Bermuda** at Vickers-Armstrong (Barrow) for the Furness Bermuda Line. Originally fitted with three funnels, she operated with her sister the **Queen of Bermuda** between New York and Bermuda, also operating cruises to the West Indies. Destroyed by fire in 1947 she then became the emigrant ship **New Australia**. In 1958 she was purchased by the Greek Line for work on the Bremerhaven-Montreal service and was eventually scrapped in 1966.*

*Union Castle's **Braemar Castle** (17,029 gross tons) was the third of a trio of liners built by Harland & Wolff in 1951/52 for the company's 'Round Africa' routes. Unlike her sisters, she travelled anti-clockwise around the continent calling at Ascension Island and St Helena en route. Although her funnel height was increased in the early 60s, making her look far more modern in appearance, she was broken up in 1966 after a very short career.*

*P&O's **Canton** was built on the Clyde by Alexander Stephen in 1938. Of 16,033 gross tons, she carried 542 passengers in two classes and operated on the company's service from the UK to Singapore and Hong Kong. The last P&O liner to be built with a black hull, she spent the war as an Armed Merchant Cruiser returning to service in October 1947. She was finally withdrawn from service in 1962 and broken up in Hong Kong.*

*Shaw Savill's **Dominion Monarch** was a product of the Swan Hunter & Wigham Richardson yard on the Tyne and entered service in 1939. A quadruple screw, diesel ship, she carried 508 First Class passengers to Wellington (New Zealand) via South Africa and Australia. Completing her final voyage in April 1962, after a brief visit to the Seattle World Fair serving as a hotel ship, she was broken up in Japan.*

*One of the more attractive of post-war liners was the **Edinburgh Castle** of 1948. Built with her sister, **Pretoria Castle**, to replace war losses at Harland & Wolff's Belfast yard, the turbine steamer was christened by Princess Margaret and carried 755 passengers in two classes. Refurbished in 1962, when her masts were shortened, she continued in service until 1976 when she was broken up in Taiwan.*

The impressive **Hanseatic** was built for the Canadian Pacific Railway's trans-Pacific service in 1930 and named **Empress of Japan**. Following the entry of Japan into the war, she was renamed **Empress of Scotland** in 1942 when she was transferred to the UK. Her sale to the Hamburg America Line followed in 1957 when she was refitted with two (rather than three) funnels. Badly damaged by fire in New York in 1966, she was towed home and later broken up.

The **Himalaya** was built in 1949 at Vickers-Armstrong's Barrow yard and was fitted with her rather unattractive smoke deflector funnel top in 1953. A two-class vessel, the 27,955 gross ton ship was originally the company's largest and fastest ship being used in her owner's service between the UK and Australia also adding a trans-Pacific link during the late 50s. Both she and her smaller near sister **Chusan** were also engaged in cruising which greatly increased towards the end of their careers. Completing service in October 1974, she was broken up in Taiwan.

The small East Asiatic Co.'s **Falstria** *(6,993 gross tons) was built in Denmark in 1941 but was only delivered in 1945 once the war had ended. An odd-looking vessel with no funnel, she was fitted with accommodation for just 60 passengers. First used on the Copenhagen-New York route, in 1949 she commenced service between Copenhagen and Bangkok. Sold to Greek owners in 1964, she was scrapped the same year in Japan.*

Built in 1930 for the Nederland Line, the **Johan van Oldenbarnevelt** *was employed to the service to the Dutch East Indies (Indonesia). In 1962 she became Greek Line's* **Lakonia** *and began cruising from Southampton in the following year. Sadly she soon gained a poor reputation and in December 1963 was gutted by fire and sank while cruising off Madeira.*

Throughout the 1950s, the pride of France was the mighty **Liberte**. Originally the great German liner **Europa**, and holder of the Blue Riband in 1931, she was acquired by the French Line to replace their **Normandie** which had been burned out while refitting in New York. Following her acquisition, she was given a thorough refit crossing the Atlantic in the opposite direction to the **Ile de France**. Replaced in service by the new **France**, she was withdrawn in 1961 and was broken up in Italy during the following year.

It is always difficult for a ship to carry the name of an illustrious forebear and this was certainly the case of Cunard's **Mauretania** of 1939 which was the first ship built for the newly formed Cunard White Star Company. She was a product of Cammell Laird at Birkenhead and only completed two trips to New York before war was declared. Accommodation was for 1,147 in three classes. Painted with a green hull in 1962, like her earlier namesake she finished her career by cruising and was scrapped at Inverkeithing in late 1965.

*The stately **Orion** of 1935 was built by Vickers-Armstrong at Barrow and was the first company liner to be painted with a buff-coloured hull, also being unusual by having only a single mast. After having completed her final return voyage from London to Sydney in May 1963, she briefly became a floating hotel in Hamburg before passing to Belgian breakers later in the year.*

*With their rather stiff and upright lines, the post-war Orient Line ships lacked something of the style of the pre-war liners. They were further spoiled when large funnel pipes were later added. Here is the **Oronsay** of 1951, south bound off the South Foreland. As with the majority of Orient Line ships, she was built by Vickers-Armstrong at Barrow. Air conditioning was fitted in 1959 and she was latterly engaged on cruising. She was broken up in Taiwan in 1975.*

The Chandris liner **Queen Frederica** *was originally the* **Malolos**, *built in Philadelphia in 1927 for the Matson Line service between San Francisco and Honolulu. Sold out of service in 1948, she became the* **Queen Frederica** *in 1954 taking up service between Piraeus and New York, later being used to carry immigrants to Australia. In early 1978 she was burned out while refitting at Perama.*

This splendid view shows the **Rangitiki** *of the New Zealand Shipping Co. She was one of a pair of sister ships built in 1929 by John Brown at Clydebank. Of a little under 17,000 gross tons, both she and her fleet companions sailed to New Zealand via the Panama Canal. Accommodation was for just 405 passengers in two classes. Retired in July 1962, she was broken up in Valencia, Spain.*

United States Line's handsome liner **America** was built in 1940 and during the 50s and early 60s she ran a joint service with her illustrious partner **United States**. Although at 26,454 gross tons, she was considerably smaller than the Blue Riband holder, there were many striking similarities between the pair. She was sold to Chandris in 1964, becoming their **Australis**.

The P&O liner **Strathnaver** is seen arriving at Tilbury. Both she and her 'white' sister ship **Strathaird** originally appeared with three funnels, the dummies being removed during their post-war refits. Products of the Vickers-Armstrong yard at Barrow in 1931/32, the turbo-electric liners carried 1,069 passengers in two classes but became one class in 1954. Latterly involved in the emigrant trade to Australia, the **Strathnaver** was scrapped in Hong Kong during 1962.

12 Roll-on/Roll-off in the Baltic

by Nick Widdows

INTRODUCTION

The Baltic Sea is basically a large lake with its only natural outlet to the wider oceans being through the Oresund or Great Belt and then the Kattegat and Skagerrak around the northern tip of Denmark. Since 1896 there has been an alternative outlet through the Kiel Canal to the mouth of the River Elbe on Germany's North Sea coast. In mediaeval times, when land transport was slow and difficult, this relatively calm and moderately sized sea formed a 'super-highway' for trade to develop and the ports of the Hanseatic League (most of which were on the Baltic) became rich and powerful in the process. After World War II, the Baltic Sea divided the free-market countries on the western side and those on the eastern side in the communist bloc. When ro-ro vessels began to replace lo-lo ships in the mid-1970s, most of the trade to switch to this method of transport flowed between North and South, with paper and other wood products flowing from Finland and northern Sweden to the markets of Western Europe, and cars, other consumer products and industrial equipment flowing north. However, following the fall of the Berlin Wall and the subsequent collapse of the Communist bloc, many more West–East traffic flows returned.

The Baltic is particularly suited to ro-ro transport as, with a very small tidal range, the creation of suitable shore infrastructure – often just a simple concrete ramp – is much easier than in the UK and other North Sea and Atlantic nations, where much more sophisticated linkspans or pontoons linked to the shore by moveable bridges are required. Some ports no longer see any regular ro-ro movements but still have the facilities, and new services could be introduced at quite short notice.

This article concentrates on ferry services which are provided primarily for the carriage of freight but does not deal exclusively with roll-on roll-off vessels limited to a maximum of 12 passengers. Such vessels tend mainly to convey trailers and containers of various sorts with a limited number of driver accompanied trucks. There are also a lot of vessels which are primarily concerned with freight but are able to accommodate more than 12 passengers – truck drivers and, in many cases car and foot passengers. The term 'ro-pax' refers to such vessels, rather than any vessel which can convey both ro-ro traffic and passengers which is an alternate use for the term.

Each operator is dealt with in alphabetical order. Ships which are provided for the conveyance of new cars and commercial vehicles are not covered since they are generally a different type of vessel. Those regular services used for paper products are mentioned as in many cases they convey general ro-ro traffic on their return journey to Finland and Northern Sweden.

*Eckero Line's **Translandia** operates a twice daily service for accompanied and unaccompanied freight between Helsinki and Tallinn. (Pekka Ruponen)*

Birka Cargo operate the **Birka Exporter** *and her sisters Birka Shipper and Birka Transporter for the Holmen paper company, to bring their products from Sweden to North European markets.(Sebastian Ziehl)*

Ro-pax vessels have since 2006 formed the mainstay of Finnlines' services between Finland and Germany, reflecting the increasing need to accommodate drivers and their trucks as well as unaccompanied trailers. Here the **Finnmaid** *approaches the German port of Travemunde. (Nick Widdows)*

In 2011, Power Line added a third vessel to their fleet in the form of the former Finnlines' vessel, **Baltica**. Finnlines had sold the vessel in 2003 and chartered her back so her transfer to a rival operator was not something that Finnlines could do anything about. (Michael Speckenbach)

The **Birka Express** and her sisters **Birka Carrier** and **Birka Trader** originally operated for Transfennica but were transferred to Finnlines in 2001. They retain Transfennica's all-white livery and the funnel markings of their owner, Birka Cargo. (Pekka Ruponen)

ANRUSSTRANS

In 2011 this Russian operator took over the train ferry and road freight service from Sassnitz to Baltijsk (Kaliningrad), which was previously operated by DFDS Seaways' *Vilnius Seaways*. The vessel used is the *Apollonia*, the former *Gotaland*, Scandlines' Trelleborg to Sassnitz, Rostock and Travemunde vessel.

BALTIC SCANDINAVIAN LINE

This Estonian operator began trading in 2005 when they acquired the *Begonia* from TransEuropa Ferries in Ostend. The former Dover-Calais/Zeebrugge *European Clearway* of Townsend Thoresen, renamed the *Via Mare* operated between Paldiski in Estonia and Kapellskar in Sweden until January 2011 when she was replaced by the larger *Kaunas*, chartered from DFDS Seaways and then, in May the even larger *Lisco Patria* took over. The service has always been available for motorists but is primarily aimed at the freight market. In October 2011, a controlling interest in the service was taken by DFDS Seaways.

DFDS SEAWAYS

Although a fairly recent entrant into the Baltic, the Danish company is now a major player. A major increase in involvement came about in 2001 when a controlling interest in the ferry operations of the state-owned Lithuanian Shipping Company (LISCO) was acquired. Trading initially as LISCO Baltic Service and then (in 2005 when the company was fully acquired) as DFDS Lisco, in 2010 the operation was rebranded as DFDS Seaways as part of a rebranding of all DFDS's ferry operations. The Kiel (Germany) to Klaipeda (Lithuania) and Karlshamn (Sweden) to Klaipeda services are operated by ro-pax type vessels, with an increasing emphasis on passenger traffic. The thrice-weekly service between Sassnitz in Germany and Klaipeda, operated by the *Vilnius Seaways*, is primarily a rail and road freight service although it is available for ordinary passengers. However, a purely freight service (previously operated by DFDS Tor Line) runs between Fredericia and Copenhagen in Denmark and Klaipeda in Lithuania using the Chinese-built *Tor Corona*. There are two circuits a week and the Danish port of Aarhus is served once per week. There is also a weekly service between Kiel and St Petersburg in Russia (with a call at Karlshamn in Sweden on the return trip) operated by the former Rotterdam-Immingham vessel *Tor Botnia*. In May 2011 a new service was inaugurated between Kiel and Ust Luga in Russia, near the Estonian border. The vessel used – the *Kaunas* – has a passenger capacity of 262 but currently this is reserved for truckers.

ECKERO LINE

Whilst some freight is carried on the company's day-trip ferry *Nordlandia* between Helsinki and Tallinn, a separate freight service is operated using the 1976-built *Translandia*. This much-travelled vessel, which has operated between Harwich and the Hook of Holland and Ramsgate and Ostend, operates two round trips per day on the 3 hour 30 minute crossing.

FINNLINES

This long-established operator – now majority owned by the Grimaldi Lines of Italy – once, with its German partner Poseidon Schiffahrt, operated a large number of ro-ro freighters on the Baltic Sea, some operating between Finnish ports and Germany and some travelling further afield, either through the Kiel Canal or round the North of Denmark. In recent years, this number has declined somewhat due to the operation of larger ships and the introduction of ro-pax vessels, which has reflected the increased demand for the carriage driver accompanied traffic (particularly to and from Russia) and also enabled the company to re-enter the passenger market, which was abandoned by the company when the gas turbine powered *Finnjet* was acquired by Silja Line partner Effoa in 1986. Five ro-pax vessels of the 500-passenger 'Finnstar class' interwork on the Helsinki-Travemunde and Helsinki-Gdynia-Rostock routes, the former on a daily basis and the latter three times per week. However, many routes continue to be operated by pure ro-ro vessels. Services operate from the Finnish ports of Turku, Rauma, Helsinki and Kotka to Rostock and Lubeck in Germany, from Helsinki to Aarhus in Denmark and from a variety of Finnish ports to Amsterdam, Antwerp, Hull, Immingham and Bilbao in Spain. The company operates a combination of owned and chartered vessels – the owned vessels being mainly modern Chinese-built vessels and the chartered vessels being three former Transfennica ships owned by Birka Shipping – the *Birka Carrier*, *Birka Express* and *Birka Trader* – and two vessels on charter from Foreland Shipping of the UK, the *Beachy Head* and *Longstone*. Two new Chinese-built vessels, the *Finnbreeze* and *Finnsea* were delivered in Spring 2011 and two more – the *Finnsky* and *Finnsun* were due later in 2011.

Finnlines also operate two shorter routes – Naantali (Finland) to Kapellskar (Sweden) branded as FinnLink, and Malmo to Travemunde branded as Finnlines NordoLink. All vessels convey accompanied freight and motorists, but the emphasis is very much on freight traffic.

HELOX LINE

HelOx Line, operated by Bore Ltd, started in December 2010 between Helsinki and Oxelösund in Sweden. Three overnight services per week are operated in each direction. The vessel used is the 1977-built *Borden*, previously operated by Mann Lines. The service is currently suspended following the sale of the *Borden* in September 2011.

HOLMEN CARRIER

The Swedish Holmen paper company operates a fleet of ro-ro vessels to convey its products to European markets. Since 2010 the service has been provided by Birka Cargo of Finland. Three vessels – the *Birka Exporter*, *Birka Transporter* and *Birka Shipper* – are deployed on services from the company's mills at Braviken and Hallstavik in Sweden to Gydnia, Lubeck, Amsterdam (all served weekly) and Chatham in the UK (served fortnightly). This is a private service for the conveyance of the company's own products (and waste paper for recycling on the northbound voyage). Commercial traffic is not normally carried on any part of the voyage.

LILLGAARD, REDERI AB

This Aland Islands-based operator runs a service between Langnas in Aland and Naantali, near Turku on the Finnish mainland. The vessel used is the 1972-built *Fjardvagen*. A six-day per week service is operated. The company also owns four small ro-ros – the *Breant*, *Hoburgen*, *Forte* and *Largo* – which are chartered out.

MANN LINES

This UK-based operator runs a weekly service from Harwich Navyard, Cuxhaven and Bremerhaven to Paldiski in Estonia and Turku in Finland. The vessel used is the 1999-built *Estraden*, time-chartered from Bore

Shipowners of Finland. Until 2010, the company operated a second vessel – the *Borden* – and both were due to be replaced by larger tonnage in 2011 – the new *Bore Sea* and *Bore Song*. However, a downturn in traffic (mainly because more traffic for Russia is going via St Petersburg and Ust Luga rather than through Finnish and Estonian ports due to recent improvement in infrastructure and efficiency) has meant that these arrangements have been postponed. Mann Lines also charters northbound capacity on the two Smurfit Kappa Group vessels *Balticborg* and *Bothniaborg* (see below).

M-REAL

Former Transfennica partner M-Real operates a twice-weekly service from Husum in Sweden to Lubeck in Germany. In addition the vessels call at Umea and Sundsvall to convey SCA Transforest traffic and at Iggesund in Sweden to pick up Holmen Paper products. They are the 1987-built *Transreel*, chartered from TransAtlantic and the 1991-built *Helena*, chartered from NorBulk Shipping of Sweden. Traffic to the UK and Benelux countries is conveyed on SCA Transforest's three vessels (see below).

NAVIRAIL

Navirail started a freight service between Helsinki and Muuga in Estonia in 2008 using the 1991-built trailer ferry *Ahtela*, the former *Finnoak* of Finnlines. In early 2010 she was replaced by the *Fellow* (formerly the *Finnfellow*) which could convey up to 100 drivers. It was planned that a second vessel would be added in early 2011 and the former Rotterdam-Harwich vessel *Transfer* (formerly the *Stena Transfer*) was expected to join the fleet. However, instead the Baltic Scandinavian Line ro-pax vessel *Via Mare* was chartered to replace the *Fellow* and the service was diverted to Paldiski. A daily service is operated.

OSTERSTROMS

This Swedish company owns a large fleet of container ships and coasters but only one ro-ro – the 1979-built trailer ferry *Festivo*, formerly part of the Holmen Carrier fleet. Since June 2011, the company has operated a thrice-weekly overnight service between Gavle in Sweden and Rauma in Finland. Also in June 2011 the company was acquired by TransAtlantic (see below) so some changes may be expected.

POLFERRIES

The long-established and still state-owned Polish operator now operates only two routes between Poland and Sweden-Swinoujscie-Ystad and Gdansk-Nynashamn. On the later route, the regular passenger vessel *Scandinavia* is backed up by the freighter *Baltivia*. This is also a much-travelled vessel, having operated between Travemunde and Trelleborg, in the Mediterranean and, as the *Dieppe*, between Newhaven and Dieppe. On the shorter Swinoujscie-Ystad route, all freight is conveyed on the passenger ferry *Wawel*.

POWER LINE

This operator is owned by Lillbacka Powerco, a global manufacturer of hydraulic crimping machines. They moved into shipping when Stena Line replaced their late 1970s 'Searunner' class *Stena Carrier* and *Stena Freighter* in 2004, previously operated between Gothenburg and Travemunde. The two ships were renamed the *Global Carrier* and *Global Freighter* respectively and a Turku-Travemunde service was launched (although initially only the

Global Carrier was used and the *Global Freighter* was chartered out). The company now operates a weekly service to Turku and twice weekly to Helsinki and a third vessel was added to the fleet in 2011 – the 1990-built ex Finnlines vessel *Baltica*.

RG LINE

This subsidised line between Vaasa in Finland and Umea in Sweden is in the hands of the 300-passenger *RG 1*. The vessel is very much of ro-pax design with limited passenger facilities and was originally operated by DSR, the East German state shipping line, as a 12-passenger freighter until additional passenger accommodation was added in 1991.

RUSSIAN FERRY LINES

This company operates between Ust Luga and Baltijsk in the Russian enclave of Kaliningrad. This route is operated by the train ferries *Baltiysk* (the former *Railship II* which operated between Turku and Travemunde for Railship and later Finnlines) and *Petersburg* (a sister vessel of DFDS's *Vilnius Seaways*).

SCANDLINES

The former Danish/German state operator, now owned by a consortium of venture capital companies, operates a number of routes, mainly in the Southern Baltic. The Helsingor-Helsingborg route carries a combination of car, bus and foot passengers and freight is not a major element. However, other routes – Rodby (Denmark)-Puttgarden (Germany), Gedser (Denmark)-Rostock (Germany), Rostock-Sassnitz-Trelleborg (Sweden), Travemunde (Germany)-Ventspils (Latvia), Travemunde (Germany)-Licpaja (Latvia) and Nynashamn (Sweden)-Ventspils (Latvia) – are more freight orientated. A pure freight service is operated between Rostock and Hanko in Finland using the former Finnlines trailer ferries *Aurora* and *Merchant*. The services to Ventspils and Liepaja employ ro-pax type vessels, although the trend has been to employ larger vessels with better passenger facilities on these routes in recent years.

SCA TRANSFOREST

This Swedish paper products company operates three ro-ro vessels. Three run between Umea (Holmsund) and Sundsvall in Sweden and Tilbury and Rotterdam. Southbound most traffic is paper, pulp and card carried on wheel-less cassettes. Northbound, the empty cassettes can be stacked on top of each other to leave space for general traffic – and to attract more traffic a call is made at Helsingborg in Southern Sweden. Three vessels are used on this service – the *Obbola*, *Ortviken* and *Ostrand* built in 1996 and 1997, until 2011 chartered from TransAtlantic but now owned by SCA Transforest. They complete two round trips every three weeks thus enabling a weekly service to be offered. They also call at two other Swedish ports – Husum to pick up M-Real traffic and at Iggersund for Holmen Paper. SCA Transforest traffic is conveyed to Germany. The three vessels were lengthened in 2000 and 2001 and purchased by the company in 2011. As mentioned above, SCA Transforest to Germany is conveyed on the service operated for M-Real.

SMURFIT KAPPA GROUP

The Smurfit Kappa Group's two ro-ro ships, the 2004-built *Balticborg* and *Bothniaborg*, are time-chartered from Wagenborg of the Netherlands. They operate on a fortnightly cycle from Pitea in northern Sweden to

*The **Caroline Russ** is now one of the oldest and smallest units in the Transfennica fleet. She is chartered from Ernst Russ of Germany. (Sebastian Ziehl)*

*Finnlines have also modernised their fleet in recent years and the 2001-built **Finnhawk** is now one of the oldest and smallest ships. Originally part of a batch of four, two have been sold and all subsequent deliveries have had an additional deck. The **Finnhawk** is seen loading in Helsinki's Vuosaari harbour. (Nick Widdows)*

Unity Line started their Swinoujscie - Trelleborg service in 2007 and the route now runs to three vessels, each operating one round trip per day, with freight as the main traffic. The 1992-built **Galileusz**, is seen here at the Swedish port. (Michael Speckenbuch)

Train ferries are less common in Northern Europe than they were, but the 1973-built **Stena Scanrail**, seen here at Gothenburg, still offers these facilities between that port and Frederikshavn in Denmark - although for how much longer remains in doubt. The vessel was converted from a conventional ro-ro ship in 1987. (Nick Widdows)

Scandlines operate two routes from Travemunde in Germany to Latvian ports. In 2011 the service to Ventspils was enhanced by the introduction of the Italian built ro-pax **Watling Street**, seen here leaving the German port. (Sebastian Ziehl)

On the Rodby - Puttgarden train ferry route, Scandlines retain the 1976-built former train ferry **Holger Danske** to carry loads which cannot be conveyed on the passenger ships. (Sebastian Ziehl)

Bremen (Germany), then Sheerness (UK), Terneuzen in the Netherlands, and Zeebrugge in Belgium. Whilst southbound the ships are normally just carrying the company's paper and card products, northbound (from Sheerness onwards) some of the capacity is chartered by Mann Lines and a call to discharge is made at Sodertalje (near Stockholm in Sweden).

STENA LINE

Following the introduction of passenger ships with much greater freight capacity on their Gothenburg-Kiel service, Stena Line ceased their Gothenburg-Travemunde freight-only service in August 2010 – although the 2004-built *Stena Freighter* was switched to provide freight back-up on the Kiel route until the second replacement ship entered service in April 2011. The two passenger vessels on the Gothenburg-Frederikshavn service are supplemented by the *Stena Scanrail*, which conveys a mixture of road and rail freight between the two ports. Space is available for up to 65 freight drivers.

SOL CONTINENT LINE

This company started a new service between Travemunde and Helsingborg in Sweden in September 2010, after Stena Line closed their Travemunde-Gothenburg service. Usually operated by the ex-Finnlines ro-ros *Antares* and *Vasaland*, the latter vessel was replaced in June and July 2011 by the Scandlines 186 driver ro-pax vessel *Ask* (the one time Sealink Dover-Dunkirk vessel *Seafreight Freeway*) to cover for refits.

TALLINK/SILJA LINE

This operator is better known for its luxurious cruise ferries operating between Sweden, Finland, Estonia and Latvia. However, two freight routes are also operated. The longest established is the Stockholm-Turku combined train ferry and road freight route operated by the *SeaWind*. Before Silja Line was absorbed by Tallink, the service was operated by subsidiary company SeaWind Line and cars were conveyed, providing a cheaper option for crossing between the two countries. Also at times a second vessel was employed on the route. The service is now branded as Tallink, reserved for freight vehicles and for the bulk of the year, only one vessel is deployed. However, during the peak summer period, when demand for car capacity on the Silja Line passenger ships is high, leaving less space for trucks and trailers, a second vessel is usually deployed. In summer 2011 this was the *Kapella*, a 1974-built vessel, once used between Folkestone and Boulogne. She operated between Turku and Kapellskar at the mouth of the Stockholm archipelago only.

A newer freight route is between Kapellskar and Paldiski in Estonia, operated by the *Regal Star* – a rather unusual vessel whose construction was started as a deep-sea ro-ro, then abandoned and completed as a short-sea ro-pax with capacity for 80 drivers. During the bulk of the year the service operates an alternate day/over-night service but in the peak summer period the service operates in both directions on most days with some day sailings.

TRANSATLANTIC, REDERI AB

As the name suggests, this company, Rederi AB TransAtlantic, operates services using lo-ro vessels (which convey a combination of ro-ro and crane-loaded freight) between Western Europe and the USA and Canada. However, they also operate a number of ro-ro services in the Baltic.

Their TransLumi Line runs from Kemi and Oulu in Finland to Lubeck in Germany and Gothenburg in Sweden. A high proportion of the traffic is for the StoraEnso paper company from their mills in Finland to their distribution hubs at Lubeck and Gothenburg, as is the TransSuomi Line which runs from Kotka to Gothenburg. At Gothenburg, some traffic is transhipped to DFDS Seaways and StoraEnso (operated by Wagenborg of the Netherlands) services to Immingham, Tilbury and Zeebrugge. The TransBothnia Line operates from Kemi and Oulu to Antwerp and Zeebrugge. The TransSuomi Line is operated by the chartered *Stena Foreteller* whilst the other two routes have a combination of the older *Tyrusland*, *Vasaland* and *Vikingland* and three vessels built in 2006 and 2007 specially for the StoraEnso traffic, the *Transpaper*, *Transpulp* and *Transtimber* (although one of the latter series is generally deployed between Gothenburg and Tilbury and Gothenburg and Zeebrugge). Their *Transreel* is chartered to M-Real (see above).

TRANSFENNICA

Transfennica was established by a consortium of paper manufacturers and its main business was, and is, the conveyance of such products from Finland to the markets of western Europe, whose demand for paper and card continues to grow. In 2006, the company was acquired in its entirety by Spliethoff Bevrachtingskantoor of the Netherlands. The acquisition followed an abortive attempt by Finnlines to take over the company which was blocked by the competition authorities. The network is very similar to Finnlines (albeit strictly freight only), with regular services from a variety of Finnish ports (plus St Petersburg in Russia and Paldiski in Estonia) to Germany, Poland, Belgium, the UK and Spain. The port of Hanko is the hub of the operation but Rauma and Hamina are also served. Like Finnlines, perhaps to an even greater extent, the carriage of goods in road trailers is matched by the use of ISO containers, some loaded on small wheeled 'Mafi' trailers, some on wheel-less cassettes and a high proportion crane-loaded onto the vessels' weather decks.

Before the Dutch company took over, all vessels were time chartered. Soon after acquiring full control, the new owners placed an order with the New Szczecin Shipyard (SSN) of Szczecin, Poland for nine vessels of a unique design for a European short-sea ro-ro operator. The unusual feature was that the trailer decks do not extend the full length of the vessel but end at the front of the accommodation block and bridge. Forward of this is a large hold where several layers of ISO containers can be stacked in the manner of a container ship. Before the last two vessels were built, the yard went into liquidation, so only seven vessels were delivered. The remainder of the fleet consists of time-chartered vessels from a variety of companies – Ernst Russ of Germany, Bore Shipowners of Finland and Stena RoRo of Sweden.

TRANSRUSSIA EXPRESS

TransRussia Express is jointly operated by Finnlines Deutschland GmbH of Germany (wholly owned by Finnlines of Finland) and JSC Baltic Transport Systems of Russia. There are three departures per week between Lubeck and St Petersburg, with intermediate calls at Ventspils and Sassnitz, each ship having a slightly different calling pattern. Vessels are all supplied by Finnlines and consist of the *Transeuropa*, *Translubeca* and *Transrussia*. The last of these three was originally the *Finnhansa*, which was the lead vessel of the 'Finnhansa' class, which before the arrival of the 'Finnstar' class ro-pax vessels in 2006 operated the daily service between Lubeck and Helsinki. The ships can convey up to 90 passengers, although these will tend to be mainly Russian truck drivers.

TT-LINE

A large amount of freight is conveyed in TT-Line's passenger ships which, with each succeeding generation have become more freight orientated. The Travemunde-Trelleborg route also employs two ro-pax vessels – the *Nils Dacke* and *Robin Hood* – which are limited to 300 passengers, although these normally also carry motorists and foot passengers. However, at weekends one of these craft operates a service to Helsingborg, further along the Swedish coast and this is restricted to freight vehicles and their drivers.

UNITY LINE

Polish Steamship Company-owned Unity Line has expanded greatly over the last ten years. As well as the passenger vessels *Polonia* and *Skania*, the company operates five freight vessels, although all are available to ordinary passengers. On the Swinoujscie-Ystad (Sweden) route the two train ferries *Jan Sniadecki* and *Kopernik* provide freight back-up to the two passenger ships. The former was built for the route, whilst the latter was originally the East German state shipping line's *Rostock*.

On the Swinoujscie-Trelleborg (Sweden) route, which started in 2007, three sailings per day are operated by the ro-pax vessels *Galileusz*, *Gryf* and *Wolin* which were all acquired second-hand.

UPM-KYMMENE SEAWAYS

Previously a part-owner of Transfennica, the Finnish paper company UPM-Kymmene now conveys the bulk of its traffic on its own ships, most operated on its behalf by Finnish company Godby Shipping. A service

*TT-Line's two ro-pax vessels **Nils Dacke** and **Robin Hood** provide freight back-up to the two passenger vessels between Travemunde and Trelleborg and also operate the weekend service to Helsingborg. (Sebastian Ziehl)*

from Kotka and Rostock to Hull, Antwerp and Tilbury is operated by the 2007-built *Misida* and *Misana*. A service from Rauma to El Ferrol or Santander in Spain is operated by the 1998-built *Miranda* and *Mistral*. The 1990-built *Midas* operates a weekly service between Rauma and Gydnia and the Birka Shipping-owned *Baltic Excellent* of 1995 together with the 1998-built German-owned *Polaris* provide a service from Rauma and Kotka to Amsterdam and Rouen.

*The **Via Mare**, originally the **European Clearway** of European Ferries, inaugurated Baltic Scandinavian Line's service between Paldiski and Kapellskar in 2005. In April 2011 she was chartered to Navirail, operating between Helsinki and Paldiski, and enabling this company to start taking accompanied freight. (Pekka Ruponen)*

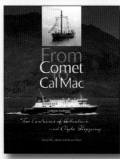

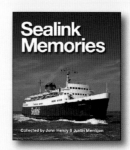